PREACHING & TEACHING
The Whole Counsel of GOD

Pastor Wayne B. Murdock

[Cover design by DIRECT GRAPHICS]

10 9 8 7 6 5 4 3 2 1

Printed in the United States of America

Published by **BLACK** Inc. Book

D e d i c a t i o n

I would like to dedicate this book of sermons, with solemn appreciation, to Mrs. Juanita Donavan Dunn, a retired schoolteacher who inspired me over eight to ten years ago to select certain sermons and have them published. I recall Mrs. Dunn saying to me, when I was appointed to her church that my sermons were enriching and insightful, and that she was collecting them. This in turn, sparked in me the interest to undertake this arduous journey to more diligently and consciously preach and teach the whole counsel of God. The bible says, "How can they hear without a preacher." The messages we preach and teach speak to the lives of people. I feel indebted to Mrs. Dunn for challenging me, as well as inspiring me, to compile selected sermons that demonstrate that I have tried over the years to preach and teach the whole counsel of God. I pray and trust that God will allow these messages to speak to others who will read them to see that God's word is true and speaks to the human condition.

Acknowledgments

I would like to extend my heartfelt gratitude to Ms. Patricia Eckles, to whom I am deeply indebted, for compiling the manuscripts of sermons I selected to be published, and formatting them to be read and edited. God allowed you to be available to assist me in making this dream of mine come to pass.

I would like to acknowledge my mentor, Dr. Gardner C. Taylor who made himself available to me for Godly counsel when my ministry in the pastorate took a one hundred and eighty degree turn in nineteen ninety-eight. Dr. Taylor, I feel indebted to you for your willingness to listen to me when I have been discouraged emotionally, mentally, physically and spiritually distraught. When my father in ministry, the Reverend John H. Partee, who had been my confidant and spiritual advisor health begin to decline and he was no longer physically capable of counseling me, you were there. When I have needed insight on a particular passage of scripture you have been there to share your wisdom and insight. Your preaching and teaching have enriched my life and ministry and have enabled me to study more ardently to show myself approved, a workman needing not to be ashamed, but rightly dividing the word of truth.

I would like to express my appreciation to the members of Assemblies of Christ Church, who have sat under my preaching and teaching for the past ten years we have journeyed together. I would like to express my deep appreciation to Dr. Walter E. Fauntroy for enriching my life and ministry; giving me a greater sense of the preaching and teaching of the gospel as it speaks to the human condition. The times we have shared together, for me, have been an invaluable experience.

I would like to acknowledge my mother, Ruth M. Murdock, who has been a tower of strength and the wind beneath my wings over the years. Your inner strength and tenacious spirit have strengthened me as well as motivated and sustained me during the difficult times in my life. Your words of wisdoms often remind me that I must continue to keep going and not give in or give up.

Finally, I would to acknowledge my daughter Leah, who has had a most profound impact on my life down through the years. Leah, you have challenged my spiritual and moral footing, first as a father and second as a minister of the gospel. You have given me reason to live during the times in my life when the odds were against me and it did not matter to me whether I lived or died. But hearing you say "daddy" made me realize that you needed me and I needed you. I thank God for being blessed to have a daughter like you; one that loves God and desires to be used by Him.

Every rich blessing on you

Love,

Believe it to be me, your Dad

F o r e w o r d

Since the tragic assassination of our beloved Dr. Martin Luther King, Jr., I have been in search of a generation of young black men and women who would say, on their watch, what we in Martin's generation said on ours. We said, "Not on our watch." Not on our watch will we be humiliated by "for white only signs" that give public sanction to the idea that we are not equal to, that we are less than, that we can never amount to very much.

Because of that generation, young black men and women served their "present age, their mission to fulfill." We made what Dr. King called great "Strides toward Freedom" on their watch. What was our mission? It was to leave the world a better place than the one our parents brought us to; and we did. We gave the world great new epochs of courage and dignity, as the patter of our feet became the thunder of the marching men of Joshua who caused the walls of racial separation by law to "come tumbling down."

As I said, however, since the tragic assassination of our beloved Dr. Martin Luther King, Jr., I have been in search of a generation of young black men and women who would say on their watch what we in Martin's generation said to men and women of conscience, of every race, creed and color, on ours. I have longed for a generation in the present age that would say, "Not on our watch" will you get us high on pot, pornography and promiscuity and have us acting like Snoop Doggie Dogs and Little Bow Wows. Our goal is to pay our debt to the past by placing the future indebt to us for what we did in our effort to end the barbarism of war, the decadence of racism and the scourge of poverty "in the present age."

In Pastor Murdock, I feel and believe I have found that generation. His capacity and passion in this book of sermons to "tell the truth in love" and to get us to "face reality with courage" is both inspiring and instructive. I pray that your journey through these well developed and thought provoking messages will empower you in your effort to stand your watch to *"Serve the Present Age, Your Calling to Fulfill, O may it all Your Powers Engage to Do the Master's will."*

The Reverend Congressman Walter E. Fauntroy

Pastor Emeritus

New Bethel Baptist Church

Washington, D.C.

Member of Congress
        1971-1991

P r e f a c e

The objective and goal of these selected sermons I have written and preached over the past twenty-seven years of my ministry have been an effort to preach and teach the whole counsel of God. The word of God is not unilateral but holistic in its revelation. The word of God speaks truth to every area of the human condition. The gospel we proclaim is not a disembodied gospel. It gives us hope beyond this life, but it also gives us a faith that is relevant and speaks to all areas of our lives. The word of God speaks to us in times of joy, sorrow, and death. The gospel tells us that God was willing to give us His best in giving us His son Jesus Christ, who was willing to come to us when we could not go to Him. The hope and the goal of each of these messages is to show how the word becomes flesh, (i.e.) real and dwells among us in truth and in power. These sermons are the distillations of my challenging and growing years in the Assemblies of Christ Church pulpit and other pulpits I have served over the past twenty-seven years. There are those living and those that have exchanged time for eternity that have encouraged me, who have reminded me that my messages have helped them establish their faith in Jesus Christ and has enlarged their vision of God.

"For I have not shunned to declare unto you the whole counsel of God." Acts 20:27

Wayne B. Murdock

Salisbury, NC

Table of Contents

1

A Biblical Understanding of Fatherhood

(Malachi 4:1-6)

Unknown, to many men who become fathers, is that fatherhood is a calling, as is motherhood. When we look at fatherhood we must first look at the fatherhood of God. There is a Father who is our God and is responsible for everything that He created. God who created everything has left His imprint of fatherhood on everything He created. The word family comes from the Greek word *patria*, which means father. Fatherhood did not begin on earth, it began in heaven. Fatherhood goes back to the fatherhood of God. When God presented Jesus, He presented Him by saying, "This is My beloved Son hear ye Him." God's purpose for sending Jesus, His Son into the world was not only to redeem us, save us, but also to ultimately bring us back to the Father. When we look at the human implication of Father, we see that every father represents God. The external character and nature of God is that of a father. A good father is the most God-like person a man can become or be.

Most men succeed today in their professions but fail as fathers. David was a great king, but he was a poor and bad example of a father. Evangelist Billy

Sunday was a great soul winner for the Kingdom of God, but he failed as a father. He was once asked how he felt having won many souls for the kingdom of God, his reply was he felt like a failure because he had won others for Christ but his family was going to hell, because he had failed as a father. A father has three roles to fulfill in his home: priest, prophet and king. As priest, the father goes to God on the behalf of his family and intercedes to God for his family. As a prophet, he represents God to his family and speaks to his family the oracles of God. He brings forth the word of God to his family. As a king, he governs his family on the behalf of God. As king, he protects and provides for his family. He leads with his head, loves with his heart and serves with his hands. When a father fails to fulfill his duties in the home, the children go into captivity. God told Moses to tell the fathers of Israel that if they failed to walk in His way, they would not enjoy their children, for they shall go into captivity. When we look at our world today, millions of our children have gone into captivity because fathers have failed to fulfill their duties. Many men and women today are being held captive by drugs, satanic activities, illicit sex, and addiction to the internet, cults, self-mutilation, body piercing and tattoos.

In many cases when the father is out of place, his family suffers. Fathers must understand that they represent God as priest, prophet, and king. When God created man He made him for a particular purpose. The inherent purpose within all men is fatherhood. Being a father is rooted in God's image because God is our father. The Hebrew word for father is "*Abba*" meaning father, daddy. And, the Greek word is

"*Pater*" meaning father.

The first word that helps to describe father is "source". The father is to be the source and sustainer of what he is called to do. The father is not only the source but also upholds, sustains and maintains his family. The father is the spiritual director that motivates, initiates, and gives his family a vision. Fathers must gain knowledge and understanding from the word of God so they can lead their families with wisdom, knowledge, integrity, and confidence. The father is the source that sustains, protects, nourishes, and provides identity for his family.

The highest honor a man can have in the eyes of God is father. Fatherhood is the ultimate work of a man. Fatherhood is honorable but brings tremendous responsibility. A man, who is physically strong, but weak as a father, is not God's man. To be strong and eloquent in words, but silent, and neglects to teach his household the Word and precepts of God, is not a father. The measure of a man's success is directly related to his effectiveness as a Godly father.

There are seven functions of fatherhood. The **first function** of fathering is sustaining his family. A father realizes that our heavenly father is his source; therefore the father knows that he must be the source and sustainer of his family. Fatherhood should not be entered into lightly. In our society too many women are called upon to do a father's job. Since God created man, man has separated himself from God and his family. We have too many fathers who are out of position and place in their homes. When the father is out of place he cannot sustain his family. When a father is out of place more than he is in place his family suffers. When fathers are out of place more than they are in place they cannot protect, guide nor lead their family. A father's presence helps to sustain his family. When the family knows that the father is always going to be there it helps to ease the tension or stress that families often incur.

The **second function** of the father is nurturer. Most fathers today fail to nurture their families. To nurture means to lead and guide your family. So many young men today go astray early in their lives because they don't have responsible fathers to nurture them. To nurture means to spend time training and equipping the siblings to deal with life's pressures regarding the things that so often deceive them, such as their friends. (Proverbs 22:5), says, "Train up a child in the way that he should go and when he is old he will not depart from it." When I was a prison chaplain I often counseled with inmates who stated that they had grown up in a home where their fathers expected the mother to teach them everything. Many stated that they failed and made mistakes because their father did not teach them about life or never had time for them. Some stated that their father provided for them but did not nurture them. R&B rap artists are influencing most young men today who are without fathers. I once heard a young man in foster care make the comment that if he had his father he would not have made some of the mistakes he had made and done some of the things that he had done. The young man realized that he needed his father.

The **third function** of a father is protector. He is to protect his family from danger at all times. Some fathers will leave their families unprotected by chasing a dollar or running with the boys. The late movie star, Carroll O'Connor, lived and died with regrets about neglecting and failing to protect his son from the evils of the world. He stated he made his career more of a priority than his family and not being there to nurture and protect his son, his son got with the wrong crowd needing attention, died of an overdose of drugs. The father as husband in the home is the band that reaches around his family to protect it from danger. He not only provides; he defends his family from outside dangers. The father is to watch over his family as a watchman. I remember when my daughter was in high school. She called me one evening and informed me that some guys at her school were harassing her and wanted to know if I would come to her school. The next day I made myself available to go to her school. When I arrived she showed me who the guys were and I addressed them regarding the matter. She informed me later that she no longer had problems with the guys harassing her. The father's role is to protect his family.

The **fourth function** of a father is teacher. If the father takes the responsibility to become the teacher and instructor in his home, he will attract God's favor and blessing. Fathers cannot expect schoolteachers to teach their children morals and values. That is not what they are paid to do. (Deuteronomy 6:6-9) says, "Thou shalt teach them," meaning the children, "when thou shalt rise up and when you lie down." Whatever the father teaches will be birthed through the mother to the children and the children's children. The father is to establish a spiritual legacy for his family. The fathers in the Old Testament were commanded to teach, "Hear O Israel, the Lord our God is one, and thou shalt love the Lord thy God with all thine heart, with all thy soul, and with all thine strength, and thy neighbor as thyself." In Paul's letter to the Ephesians, the sixth chapter, verse 4 says, "And you fathers, do not provoke your children to wrath, but bring them up in the training and admonition of the Lord." The father is to be the spiritual director of the home.

The **fifth function** of a father is disciplinarian. Discipline is not punishment. Discipline takes teaching to the next level. Discipline is training. (*Proverbs 22:5*) says, "Train up a child in the way he should go, and when he is old he will not depart from it." The problem with many of our children today is that we train and teach them about things of the world, but fail to train and teach them about the things of God. I once asked a group of young men regarding their view or understanding of God and the church, (I quote) "Too many people in the church are hypocrites" one stated, and that he did not care anything about God. He only came to church because he was forced to come. This is an indictment on fathers. Fathers have failed to train up their children in the way they should go. A young man once said to me that he learned how to hustle from watching his dad. He stated that his father was a hustler so he grew up hustling like his father. He stated that his father never took him to church he only went with his mother or grandmother.

The **sixth function** of fathering is being a leader. Being the leader of your family does not mean as father you are superior, better, or greater than the woman. It means his first responsibility and accountability is to his family. The father is to lead with his head, love with his heart and serve with his hands. Fathers as leaders are first and foremost servants like Jesus Christ. Fathers cannot lead until they first learn how to serve. Fathers need to say more than, "I'm the head of my house." They must remember that being the head brings with it the responsibility to preserve, protect, nourish, and guide the family. In order for the father to be a good a leader he must first learn how to follow the Leader, Jesus Christ. Jesus said, "He that would be great among you let him be your servant." A father does not lead necessarily by what he says, but by the example he sets for his family to follow.

The **seventh** and final **function** of fatherhood is provider. The father is the visionary for his family. Not only is he the visionary, he is the provider. He provides a vision for his family. He outlines goals for his family. (*1 Timothy 5:8*) says, "But if anyone does not provide for his own, and especially those of his household, has denied the faith, and is an infidel, unbeliever." Fathers, who have children even if they are not married to the child's mother, have an obligation to provide for the child. If a father fails to provide, the bible likens him as an infidel, not a believer. You bring disgrace and dishonor to the Christian faith and to fatherhood.

God holds fathers accountable because fathers represent God who is our heavenly Father. When fathers step up and fill their God given position as fathers, then God will turn the hearts of the fathers to the children and turn the heart of the children to the fathers.

I was counseling a family once whose young teenage daughter had gotten out of control and the parents had to involve the juvenile court system for help in an effort to save and protect their daughter from danger. In counseling the family, the father did not want to participate in the family's therapy sessions. After a few months had passed there was some improvement with the teenager's behavior. Toward the end of the therapy sessions I recommended to her court counselor that she not go to a level four facility but remain in the home. The court counselor had recommended her for a higher level of care in a level four facility against my recommendation. The family's attorney later contacted me concerning my position. I still recommended that she remain with her family. In the court room the father asked the judge if he could speak and the judge agreed. The father stated to the judge that the therapy sessions had helped his daughter; but he had not involved himself. He had not participated in the treatment as he should have, but if the judge would allow his daughter to remain in the home he would take more responsibility as a father. He would become a better father for his daughter, because her behavior was due largely to his failure to spend more time at home. He was working overtime every week. The judge, upon my recommendation, honored the father's request.

"He shall turn the hearts of the fathers to the children and the hearts of the children to the fathers." "If my people who are called by My name will humble themselves and pray and seek My face, turn from their wicked ways then I will hear from heaven, and forgive their sin and heal the land." God can turn the hearts of fathers to their children if fathers will repent. God can call the prodigal son or daughter home if fathers will seek God's face. God will save the family if fathers will pray for their families. God can bring a wandering child home if fathers will humble themselves - make their families a priority. God will redeem the family if fathers will turn to Him and trust Him to bring it to pass.

2

Building On a Firm Foundation

(Psalm 11 & I Corinthians 3:5-17)

The story is told about a man who had a crack in his wall. He called the man who plastered walls with a plaster solvent. One month later the man noticed that his wall had another crack in the same place or area; at least he thought it was the same place or area. He called the plasterer back and said to him, "I paid you to fix this crack in my wall and the crack has come back." The man examined the wall and tried to fix the crack but could not. The plasterer told the man that he would need to get an engineer to come and look at the structure and foundation of his house.

The man hired an engineer to come and look at the structure of his house to determine why his walls were cracking. The engineer told the man after he had examined the structure that the foundation his house was built on had a crack in it. It would do no good to fix the cracks because the foundation was cracked and every time the ground settled after a hard rain the foundation would shift and cause cracks in the walls. Until the foundation was repaired, the walls would continue to crack.

This story is a parable of life. If there are cracks in different areas of our lives it could be because there's a crack in our foundation. If the foundation of our lives is not solid there will be a ripple affect or chain reaction in every area of our lives. The word of God is the foundation for our lives and the foundation has been laid for our lives.

But, *if the foundations are destroyed, what can the righteous do?*

When we look at the breakdown and dysfunction of the family, there is obviously a crack in the foundation of the structure of the family. Teenage pregnancies, juvenile delinquency, crime in high schools, and teenagers carrying weapons to school out of fear or retaliation. All of these social, emotional, and mental pathologies stem from there being a crack in the foundation of the family and this country.

We cannot build a family on a solid foundation without Jesus Christ. Fathers and Mothers need to know their roles and responsibilities as parents. God has given the blue print for the structure of the family. Husbands love your wives; wives honor your husbands. Children obey your parents. The man is the head of the wife; he is not to be a dictator. He is to lead with his head and mind, love with his heart and serve with his hands. Wives are to submit to their husbands out of love, not fear. Wives are to be a helpmate, not a weight.

Parents, train up a child in the way that he should go. The television teaches our children more than parents teach them. Two different generations cannot raise the same child. We live in a society where each generation is different. What has worked for one generation may not work for another. A family without a spiritual base has no solid foundation. Paul says, "Foundation can no man lay than that which is laid which is Jesus Christ."

A family lacking a spiritual base is subject to cracks in their foundation. If the foundation of our families has a crack there will be cracks in other areas of the family.

Most people marry for convenience and not because the bible says marriage is honorable. Many people marry for security, not love. Some marry looking for happiness. If you are not secure with whom you are as a person and happy with yourself, there is no guarantee you will find happiness in your marriage or mate. So many people marry for the wrong reasons. Some men and women marry due to loneliness and some marry because they do not want to be alone.

The family is the basic institution of society. However we fail when the family is based on a sociological frame of reference instead of a biblical or spiritual frame of reference. When the family is out of order every thing else is affected. If the foundation of the family is cracked, everything else will be affected or impacted in a negative way.

The church is the family of God, made up of family units. A congregation is no stronger than the families that make up the church. If the families are not in order, the church cannot be in order. The family should be a reflection of the church and the church should reflect the family. God is a God of order.

If parents are without a spiritual base, the children will grow up without a spiritual base. If parents do not value the church, children grow up not valuing the church. The bible says, "train up a child in the way that he should go, and when he is old he will not depart." *(Proverbs 22:6)*.

There is a difference between raising and training. The Bible says we are to train our children, not raise. We raise animals but we train children. From a biblical perspective train means to instruct, develop, shape and equip. Most parents raise their children but they do not train them. We must train them to think, to be responsible, to take responsibility for their actions and to be industrious.

If we look at the foundations of this country we discover that nothing is stable. *(Psalms 82:5)* says, "All the foundations of the earth are shaken and out of order." The dysfunction of the order of things can be traced back to the family. Problems in schools can be traced to the breakdown in the family. Crime can be traced back to the family. Gangs emerge as a result of young men and women not having a sense of belonging to their family, so they gain a family by forming an alliance and allegiance to a group that gives them a sense of family - making them feel that they belong to something. Psychologist Maslow's hierarchy of needs, states, that one needs to feel a sense of belonging to feel self fulfilled and to reach self actualization.

If the foundations are destroyed, what can the righteous do?

For no other foundation can anyone lay than that, which is laid, which is Jesus Christ. How can we build a family on a firm foundation? What can we do to eliminate the cracks in the walls of the family? How can we eliminate cracks in the church?

The **first suggestion** we must consider and understand is that God has set the foundations of the world. The Apostle Paul says, "For no other foundation can anyone lay than that which is laid, which is Christ Jesus." The Bible tells us that in the beginning God has laid the foundations of the world.

The founding fathers were theists; they believed in God and realized this when they wrote the Declaration of Independence. They were not Christians but they believed in God. Many people are theist, they believe in God but they are not Christians. It is not enough to believe in God and it is to believe God. The founding fathers of this country believed in a creator and they wrote the Declaration of Independence using these words: "We hold these truths to be self evident that all men are created equal and are endowed by their creator with certain unalienable rights. Among these are life, liberty and the pursuit of happiness." However, the declaration acknowledges that there is a creator but does not uphold the tenets of the declaration.

If we are to eliminate the cracks in the walls of the family we must be sure we are building on the right foundation. The declaration of independence is not the foundation for the family. The foundation for the family has already been laid in the word of God. The problem is that most people in the church do not read the word of God.

God told Joshua, that this book of the law, meaning the Bible, "Shall not depart out of your mouth, but you shall meditate on it day in and day out, that you may observe to do all that is written therein, then you will make your way prosperous, then you will have good success." For no other foundation can no man lay than that which is laid, which is Christ Jesus.

The **second suggestion** we must consider is to

be sure we are building our families and the church on a firm foundation. The plan God has laid for the family and the church in the word of God. As Christians we have instructions as it relates to the family and the church. The problem is that we ignore God's plan and want to do it our way. We hear God's word preached and taught but we reject His word. (Proverbs 14:12) says "There is a way which seems right unto man, but his way in the end thereof is death." (Matthew 7:24) says, "Therefore whosoever hears these sayings of mine and does them is likened to a wise man who built his house on a rock." So often we want to make a family everything that God has not intended it to be. Whenever we try to make a family or the church something God has not intended it to be, it is like the man who built his house on the sand, when the storm and strong winds came it blew and destroyed the house.

The Apostle Paul says in *(1 Corinthians 3:12-13),* "If anyone builds on the foundation gold, silver, precious stones, wood, hay and straw, each man's work will be revealed; for the day will declare it, because it will be revealed by fire. The fire will test each one's work, of what sort it is." A family has to be built on love, honesty, faithfulness, respect, and communication. Valuing one another and affirming one another's worth and value within the family is needed. The church is built on prayer, faith, and love for God and love for one another. It is built on service, stewardship of time, talent, tithes and spiritual gifts. The church is not a container that we use just for Sunday school, bible study, and worship. The church has a calling to fulfill, and a mission to accomplish. It is to seek the lost, to win souls for Jesus Christ, to proclaim liberty to the captives, and to open the eyes of the blind. The church is not the building, but the building is where the church meets. Where the spirit of the Lord is there is the church.

If the foundations be destroyed, what can the righteous do?

The **third and final suggestion** we must consider and know to build the family on a firm foundation is that God is still in charge of his people. The foundation God has lain for the church is sure. *(2 Timothy 2:19)* says, "Nevertheless the foundation of God stands sure; the Lord knows those that are His." *(Psalm 11:4)* says, "The Lord is in His Holy temple, the Lord's throne is in heaven."

The Lord tests the righteous. The people of God are sometimes so heavenly minded they are no earthly good. The church, the people of God, becomes too comfortable sometimes and concerns itself only with its needs and neglects the needs of others. The church has been guilty of setting back and condoning many of the sins in our country. God will test the works of the church. Some years ago the Southern Baptist Convention made a public statement that they were wrong for condoning slavery. In the book of Revelations chapters two and three, the word came to the churches stating, "I know thy works." God knows if the works of the church is worthy of praise or condemnation. He knows if we have left our first love. God knows if the church is hot or cold or lukewarm. God knows if the church has a name that it lives but it is dead. God knows if the church is doing the works of Satan. God knows if the church is being persecuted for righteousness. God knows all about us.

(2 Chronicles 7:14) says, "If my people who are

called by my name will humble themselves and pray, and seek my face, and turn from their wicked ways, then I will hear from heaven and forgive their sin and heal their land." Sometimes the church needs to humble itself and repent of its sin. The church is guilty of the sin of self-righteousness and the sin of omission and commission. But nevertheless the foundation of the church is sure. God knows them that are His and that will stand for what's right. Jesus said, "He would build His church and the gates of hell would not prevail against the church against it." In the early church's beginning, the church was met with many evil attacks but the church prevailed.

The story is told about a turbulent storm that came one night and destroyed many homes. There were many trees that were uprooted by the storm. But there was an old oak tree that was leaning but it had not been uprooted as other trees had been. It was strange to others that the oak tree had survived the storm. A geologist was called to inspect the tree and they dug deep into the ground around the oak tree and they discovered that the oak tree's roots were wrapped around a big rock and the rock was firmly planted in the ground. Well the foundation of the oak tree was anchored by the rock. If the foundation of the family is to survive the storms of life that leave cracks, it must be grounded and rooted in the rock of ages. This rock is Jesus; the stone that the builders rejected. This rock is indestructible, this rock is the foundation, and this rock is a rock in a weary land.

In every high and stormy gale my anchor holds within the veil. On Christ the solid rock I stand, all other ground is sinking sand. I dare not trust the sweetest frame but wholly lean on Jesus name.

3

A RESURRECTION FAITH

(John 11: 18-27)

The resurrection is about life after death and victory over death. Job asked the question, "If a man dies shall he live again?" The answer to this question was not answered until Jesus came. Jesus said to Martha regarding the question of death as it related to the death of Lazarus her brother, "That whosoever lives and believes in Me though he may die he shall live. And whosoever lives and believes in Me shall never die." Death for the Christian is not final if we believe in the resurrection of Jesus Christ; that's why Jesus said to Martha, "Your brother will live again."

In each of these two verses Jesus emphasized the importance of one believing. What we believe, whether it is true or false, is powerful. Jesus said, "If thou canst just believe all things are possible." How we live is based to some degree on what we believe. We see throughout the New Testament each time Jesus encountered an individual who needed healing, He would always stress the importance of believing and having faith. In this eleventh chapter of John, which is our text, the word "believe" is mentioned six times.

The resurrection is a bodily experience; a spirit does not have a body. *(1 Peter 3:18)* says, "For Christ also hath once suffered for sins, the just for the unjust, that He might bring us to God, being put to death in the flesh, but quickened by the spirit." The body and the flesh is what dies, the spirit does not die. The Spirit goes back God. We cannot see a Spirit but we can see the works of the Spirit in a bodily form. It was the spirit that raised Christ from the dead. The Spirit is what raises the body.

The Spirit is what gives life to the body; therefore the body without the spirit is dead. When we talk about the resurrection we are talking about a bodily resurrection based on what one believes. Jesus made it very clear to Martha that the resurrection of her brother and the resurrection itself was a matter of believing. As believers we must live with a resurrection faith. We must believe in the power of His resurrection. There are three dimensions of a resurrection faith.

The **first dimension** of a resurrection faith is that it must first be personal. It takes more than hearing the Word of God, although faith comes by hearing, and by hearing the Word of God. Faith is acting on what one believes as a result of what one has heard and seen. Jesus asked Martha after He had told her that He was the resurrection and the life, "Believeth thou this?" Resurrection faith has to be personalized and internalized. There are some things we must know and believe regardless of the circumstances.

It was not enough for Jesus to tell Martha that He was the resurrection and the life; she had to believe He was who He said He was. Job said, "I know that my redeemer lives." John says, "We speak that we know and testify to that which we have seen." Martha's reply was, "Yes lord: I believe that thou art the Christ, the Son of God which should come into the world." She believed in the general resurrection but she needed to believe that Jesus was the resurrection in the present tense as well as the future tense. Jesus was challenging her to believe in the present tense that He was the resurrection and she did not have to wait for the general resurrection, which would come in the future. She needed to believe who He said He was as it concerned life and death. Martha knew He could raise Lazarus, for she had stated earlier, "But even now I know that whatever You ask God, God will give You." She knew that He was able to resurrect Lazarus, her brother, right then if He would ask God. If our faith is to be a resurrection faith it has to be personal.

The **second dimension** of a resurrection faith is that it must be productive, meaning alive and lived. A resurrection faith has to be lived in the present. We live in the power of His resurrection. Jesus said because I live ye shall live also. Resurrection deals with the physical, the spiritual and the natural. God can restore life and health to us in the present. God does not wait until we die to resurrect our lives; He does it while we live if we believe. Jesus said in *(John 6:63)*, "The words I speak unto you, they are spirit and they are life."

I went to visit my father in the ministry who was confined to a nursing home. On one occasion, he appeared to be in a comatose state and he appeared to be unconscious. One of the amazing things about Reverend John H. Partee was that he knew the bible very well and certain scriptures throughout the bible he knew verbatim. When it appeared that he was unconscious and could not speak, I begin to quote the Twenty-third psalm. As I begin to quote the Twenty-third psalm he began to respond and quote the psalm along with me. When I would quote one verse he would quote the other part of the verse. As I continued to quote the psalm he rose *up* in his bed and became alive. Jesus said, "My words are spirit and life." All we have to do sometimes is speak the word and when we speak the word we must believe what we are speaking.

The Centurion's daughter was sick. He went to Jesus and said to him, "You don't have to go where she is all you have to do is speak the word and she will be healed." God's word brings life and healing to our lives. God's word brings resurrection power to our lives. A resurrection faith speaks the word and the lame walks; a resurrection faith speaks the word and the sick gets well; a resurrection faith speaks the word and the wounded is made whole. A resurrection faith speaks the word and the prisoner is set free.

The **third** and final **dimension** of a resurrection faith is that it must be prophetic. What we mean by prophetic is that what has been spoken will come to pass at the appointed time. Martha's faith in the resurrection was more prophetic at first than it was personal. She said to Jesus I know my brother will rise again; he will rise in the general resurrection. The general resurrection is where all that have died in Christ will be raised together. That statement was prophetic, she believed in the resurrection - when the dead in Christ would all rise.

The Sadducees did not believe in the resurrection, they believed when you die that was the end of life. But the Apostle Paul said, "If only in this life we have hope, we are men most miserable, but now is Christ risen from the dead and has become the first fruits of them that sleep."

A resurrection faith that's prophetic says in the words of Job, I know that my redeemer lives and though worms destroy my body, yet in my flesh shall I see God.

A prophetic faith in the resurrection says in the words of the Apostle Paul, "We know that when this earthly house has been dissolved we have a building not made by hands."

A prophetic faith in the resurrection says, "For me to live is Christ, and to die is gained."

A prophetic faith in the resurrection says, "To be absent from the body is to be present with the Lord."

A prophetic faith in the resurrection says, "Behold I show you a mystery, we shall not all sleep but we shall all be changed in a moment, in the twinkle of an eye."

A prophetic faith in the resurrection says, "It does not yet appear what we shall be, but we know that when He shall appear we shall be like Him for we shall see Him as He is."

A prophetic resurrection faith says, "We know in part, but we shall know as we are known."

A prophetic faith says, "We know that all things work together for the good of them that love God and are called according to His purpose."

A prophetic faith says, "Weeping may endure for a night but joy comes in the morning."

A prophetic faith says; keep trusting; keep believing, keep hoping, keep watching, keep waiting. When He shall come in trumpet sound, O may I then in Him be found, dressed in His righteousness alone faultless to stand before His throne.

4

"Four Truths That Will Move a Church Forward"

As we enter each New Year as a church and as individuals, we must understand that we play a vital role and part in the things we seek to achieve. We are to set our affections on things above as well as some of the earthly things. We ought not to become so heavenly minded as we approach each New Year that we are no earthly good. Our affection for heavenly things should become stronger. Our desire and affection for God and the things of God should become stronger. All too often, we expect God to do for us the things we can do for ourselves. God will do His part, He always has and He always will. We cannot put the total responsibility on God. God works in us to do His good will and His pleasure.

However, we must acknowledge that He is our source. He is our source of life, our source of healing, and our source of strength, and our source of all spiritual and material blessings. He tells us in His word that, "Without Me you can do nothing." (St. John 15:5) God is a God that leads His people forward, not backward. The bible teaches that we are to go from strength to strength, faith to faith and glory to glory. We are never to remain static or stagnate. However, God does instruct us to wait on Him. Whenever God instructs us to wait, He has a purpose for telling us to wait. Whenever He instructs us to wait, He tells us to work while we are waiting. We are not to sit and wait for God to do everything for us. Many people, some being Christians, misunderstand what God means by waiting. Some people think God means for them to sit idly by and do nothing. When God speaks we must move forward.

Each New Year, as each new day, brings us opportunities if we are prepared to meet the challenge. If the church is to move forward and lay hold of the things that God has prepared for them that love Him, we must do certain things. If our lives are to be richer and fuller, we must do certain things. If we are to move forward this year we must do certain things. If we are to grow from the mistakes we made last year we must do certain things. If we are to lay hold to the abundant life that Jesus said He came to bring us, we must do certain things and make the necessary changes and adjustments in our lives.

The **first truth** and thing we must do to move forward each New Year, is to release the past and focus on the new. *(Isaiah 43:18)* says, "Remember ye not the former things, neither consider the old things." So many people are trapped in the past, and held prisoner by their past. All too often we spend too much time talking about the past and those things that happened to us. Some people, and many being Christians, are trapped in their past. There comes a time when we will have to let go of our past or our past will always be our present and therefore we will have no future. Many people remind others of their past and they use their past to discourage them from going forward. Until one releases their past their past will always be their present, therefore, they will have no future. The text says that we are not to remember the former things, neither are we to consider them. We are not to even think about the past. We honor the things in our past that were good and we learn from the mistakes but we keep moving forward.

Legendary basketball coach Phil Jackson, who played with the New York Knicks years ago, played with Dave Debusschere. Dave talks about a game they played together one night at Madison Square Garden where he made a bad pass to Phil and they lost the game. The next evening Dave reminded Phil that he blew the game the night before by making a bad pass to him. Phil stated to Dave, "What happened last night is over, it's behind us, let last night's game go and come out and be ready to play tonight."

We cannot allow our past to destroy what God has for us in the present. We are to release the past and focus on the future. The Apostle Paul stated, "Forgetting those things that are behind me and reaching those things that are before me." "I press toward the mark for the prize for the higher calling of God in Christ Jesus" (Philippians 3:13-14). Going forward sometimes means that we will have to press forward, which requires us to apply ourselves more.

The **second truth** and thing we must do if we are going to go move forward is to trust God for greater dimensions. *(Isaiah 54:2)* says, "Enlarge the place of thy tent, and let them stretch forth the curtains of thine habitations: spare not, lengthen thy cords, and strengthen thy stakes." We are to enlarge our territory. We are not to be satisfied where we are, and we are to enlarge our vision. We are to have a larger vision for the church as well as a larger vision for our lives. "For where there is no vision the people will perish."

So many people lack purpose and vision in their lives. God's purpose is to take His people to higher dimensions in Him. We should aim to do more for God and His work. No one should be satisfied where he or she is spiritually. We should be not only a hearer of the word but also a doer of the word. You should want to enlarge your spiritual tent. We should want our faith to take us places where we have never gone and do things for God and ourselves that we have never done. We are to call those things that be not, as though they were, (Romans 4:17).

We should seek to stretch and lengthen our faith in God; trust God to open doors and move mountains. We should strengthen the stakes of our lives. The things that hold our lives together and give us purpose and meaning, such as family, church, friends and anything that promotes the will of God we should strengthen. We strengthen the stakes of those areas with prayer, spending quality time with God and love those whom God has given us to love. All too often we fail to value the time we have with each other and we take one another for granted. Dr. Bernice King stated that one of the things she learned during the last moments with her mother, Coretta Scott King, was to value the moment and time she had with her mother before she died. We often fail to value and appreciate one another.

The **third truth** we need to grasp to move forward in our lives is the shield of faith. *(Ephesians 6:16)* tells us to take the shield of faith to quench the fiery darts of the wicked. The shield of faith is probably the most important piece of the armor we are instructed to wear. There are two different words used for shield. One is a small circular shield, shaped like a large, round flat basket. The other one is a long rectangular shield and is taken from the word door because it is shaped like a door.

The shield Paul is talking about that we must utilize is the shield of faith. This shield covers our whole body. Satan will attack our minds, our hearts, our bodies, our children, and our finances. Satan will attack any area of our lives that he can reach that is not protected. The shield of faith will cover all that we have and all that belongs to us. We need the shield of faith to protect us from negative forces. In moving forward in life we will always meet opposing forces. The forces of evil will always seek to work against the purposes of God. Faith is knowledge of the word of God, and faith comes by hearing, hearing the word of God. We have to be knowledgeable of the word of God and speak the word of faith as a shield to counteract the forces of evil. We have to fight the fight of faith.

The Apostle Paul said, "Fight the good fight of faith." (1Timothy 6:12). When the enemy tells us that we cannot achieve or be successful, faith tells us I can do all things through Christ that strengthens me. When the enemy works against us, faith tells us that no weapon formed against me shall prosper.

When we want to give up, faith tells us to be still and know that God is God and He will not allow our enemies to prevail. Faith tells us that if God be for us who can be against us. Faith tells us to stand still and see the salvation of the Lord. Faith tells us God is our sun and shield, He gives grace and glory, no good thing will He withhold from them that walk uprightly.

When we have tried and it seems that things are not going to work out, and you want to quit, faith tells us, let us not grow weary in well doing, for in due season we will reap the harvest if we faint not. Faith tells us when our patience runs out, "That though the vision tarry wait for it, for it will surely come." The shield of faith tells us, "That when the enemy comes in like a flood, the spirit of the Lord will lift up a standard against it. Our faith is the radar that sees through the fog.

The **fourth** and final **truth** that will move us forward as a church this year is to see the work of God as a labor of love. We must enjoy the journey; allow the joy of the Lord to strengthen us. We must love and enjoy the work of the Lord. We must see what we are doing in the church as a labor of love. As Christians, we must enjoy working and serving God. We must enjoy worshipping together, praying together, serving together, fellowshipping together, singing together and studying together. We cannot see the work of the kingdom as a task. We have to see it as a calling. If you have not been called to a ministry in the church you will see your work as a task and not a labor of love. The Apostle Paul stated, in *(Romans 1)*, "I am indebted, I am not ashamed of the Gospel, and I am now ready." (1Corinthians 1:9) says there is a reward for them that love God. "For it is written: Eye has not seen, nor ear heard, nor have entered into the heart of man the things that God has prepared for those that love Him." When we show God that we love Him, He will open doors that no man can open, and close doors that no man can close. He will enlarge your territory; He will make the crooked places in your life straight. He will make the rough places smooth. He will make our enemies our friends. He will prepare a table before us in the presence of our enemies. We are to serve the

Lord with gladness: come before His presence with singing, enter into His gates with thanksgiving and enter his courts with praise, be thankful unto to Him and bless his name.

5

When It Seems Your Faith is not Enough

(Hebrews 11:1-7)

When we talk about faith; we understand faith to be personal. The scriptures tell us that the just shall live by his faith. We walk by faith and not by sight. From Genesis to Revelation we are told of the importance and necessity of faith. We are told that, "Without faith it is impossible to please God. For he that would come to Him must believe, believe that He is a rewarder to them that diligently seek Him." In *(Hebrew 11:6)* we are told that, "Faith is the substance of things hoped for and the evidence of things not seen." We are told that, "faith comes by hearing, by hearing the word of God." The word of God, which is the word of faith, helps to establish our faith. The things we experience in life serve to test our faith as well as prove our faith to be authentic or synthetic. A faith untested or tried is not an authentic faith. The Epistle of James says, "Brethren counted all joy when you fall into various trials, knowing that the testing of your faith produces patience." (James 1: 2-3)

We are told according to the scriptures that we go from faith to faith, which suggests that our faith is existential, meaning that our faith is always in a state of becoming, always growing. As Christians, according to the scripture, we all have been given a measure of faith and we need to add to the measure that God has imparted to each of us. We are told that we walk by faith and not by sight. Faith is acting and practicing what we believe to be the truth. We know that faith has five dimensions. Faith is knowledge, faith is belief, faith is trust, faith is hope and faith is obedience. We read in our text the faith of the patriarchs. "By faith we understand that the worlds were framed by the word of God, so that the things, which are seen, were not made of things, which are visible." *(Hebrews 11:3)*

By faith Abel offered to God a more excellent sacrifice than Cain.

By faith Enoch was taken away so that he did not see death, and was not found.

By faith Noah being divinely warned of things not yet seen, moved with Godly fear and prepared an Ark.

By faith Abraham obeyed when he was called to go out to a place where he would receive an inheritance.

By faith Sarah herself also received strength to conceive seed, and she bore a child when she was past the age.

By faith Abraham, when he was tested, offered up Isaac, and he who had received the promise offered up his only begotten son at Mt. Moriah. All of these, by their faith, trusted God.

There comes a time in each of our lives when it seems that our faith does not work. There comes a time in each of our lives when it seems that our faith has failed us. There comes a time when it appears that our faith is not enough. There comes a time when it appears that our faith gets bogged down with doubt. It gets bogged down with feelings of uncertainty as to what we should do next. There comes a time when it appears that our faith limits what we can do. Jesus said to Peter, "Simeon, Simeon, Satan desires your soul, he desires to sift you like wheat, but I pray that your faith fail you not." There are times when we find ourselves going through the vicissitudes of life and our faith seemingly is not enough or it appears that it has failed us. There are times when we say Lord I believe, but Lord help thou my unbelief. What are we to do when it seems our faith does not work? What are we to do when it appears that our faith is not enough? What are we to do when it appears that our faith has failed us? What are we to do when it appears that our faith is not enough to get us to the next level?

Should we defect from the faith? Should we abandon our faith? Should we become apostates when we feel our faith is not enough? Should we turn back, or look back? Should we jump ship because we feel that the anchor of our faith does not hold within the stormy veil and it is not enough to keep us from drowning?

In **(I Peter 1),** it talks about faith and that we should give all diligence to add to our faith. We have stated that God has given to every man a measure of faith. The problem with some people who feel their faith is not enough is that they have not added to the measure of faith God has given them. God has deposited into each of our lives a measure of faith that will enable us to add to or build on. Each of us should have a faith bank account that we can draw from when we need God's assurance, when we face trials and difficulty. Faith tells us that God is the same today, yesterday and forever. When we are able to draw from our faith bank account it will put us in remembrance of who God is and what He has already done in our lives. When we can draw from our faith we will be able to live by our faith.

The **first thing** we must do when it seems that our faith is not enough is to add more knowledge to our faith. When your faith seems to not be enough you need to know that faith comes by hearing, hearing the word of God. God's word tells us that if we have the faith, as a grain of a mustard seed we can say to the mountain be thou removed and it shall be done; that's knowledge of the word of God. God's word tells us that "things with man are impossible but with God all things are possible to them that believe;" that's knowledge. God's word tells us that faith is the substance of things hoped for and the evidence of things not seen; that's knowledge. The apostle Paul stated, "That I know in whom I have believed and that He is to keep that which I have committed unto Him against that day." (*2Timothy1:12*). When we have Knowledge of the word of God our anchor will hold. Knowledge of the word of God tells us that God has promised never to leave us, nor forsake us, nor fail us, because He is the same today, yesterday, and forever. If God was faithful to us in the past he will be faithful to us in the present and future. As Christians we need more knowledge of God's word to keep our faith alive and operative.

The **second thing** to add to our faith when it seems that our faith is not enough is praise and thanksgiving. Sometimes we fail to thank God for what He has already done. In everything we are to give thanks for this is the will of God according to the word of God**.** We must thank God when things are going well for us, and when things appear to be going against us. God is a God of both the mountains and the valleys. David said, "Yea though I walk through the valley and shadow of death I will fear no evil for thou art with me." I will bless the Lord at all times, His praise shall continually be in my mouth. When praises go up blessings come down. "Oh that men would praise the Lord for His goodness and for the wonderful works of the children of men." God inhabits the praises of His people. I remember when my father in the ministry's child died and a few weeks after her death I went to visit him and offer my sympathy. He stated to me that he thanked God for having given him a daughter and that it just made him love the Lord more. He stated that he knew his daughter was saved and that she was with the Lord.

The **third thing** to add to your faith when it seems that your faith is not enough is prayer and fasting. The bible says in *(Luke 18:1),* "Men ought to always pray and faint not." If we would spend more time in prayer, talking to God, our faith would be enough. Charles Finney, one of the great evangelists of the twentieth century said, "Faith moves men but prayer moves God." Then there are times when we need to fast to deny the flesh and lean solely on God. In *(Mark 9)* Jesus cast a dumb and deaf spirit out of a man's son. The disciples could not cast out the dumb and deaf spirit, so the man took his son to Jesus and Jesus cast out the dumb and deaf spirit. His disciples wanted to know why they could not and Jesus replied, "This kind comes forth but by prayer and fasting." Prayer locked the jaws of the lions when Daniel was in the lion's den. Daniel prayed and fasted while in the lion's den. Paul and Silas prayed while in the Roman jail and an earthquake came, broke the chains and loosed them. When Peter was put in jail, the church began to pray and while they were yet praying Peter knocked at the door. Prayer changes things. Just a little talk with Jesus, tell Him all about your troubles.

The **fourth and final thing** to add to our faith when it seems our faith is not enough is patience. Sometimes we want to get ahead of God. Faith works within three principles, the will of God, the grace of God and the timing of God. The things we ask God for, we must first know if it's in the will of God. We have to be patient. Faith works with the grace of God. By grace ye are saved through faith. There is a relationship between grace and faith. Faith is the glove that grace is channeled through. *(Ephesians 2:8)* Faith works within the timing of God. Job said, "That in all my appointed times I will wait until my change comes." For some things, we will have to be patient and work through whatever we are going through, and in God's own time, He will bring it to past. He gave Abraham and Sara Isaac but it was in His time, not their time. Faith wins the victory but it is in God's own time. Faith can move mountains but it is in God's own time. Faith and trials work together. Trials come to produce patience, but our faith is being perfected. We cannot hurry God, He may not come when we want Him to come but He is always on time. "Though the vision tarries, wait for it, for it will surely come." They that wait upon the Lord shall renew their strength, they shall mount up with wings as eagles they shall run and shall not be weary; they shall walk and not faint. God has promised to renew our strength and faith if we wait on Him.

6

Intimacy With God

(Ephesians 2:11-13)

Our text deals with how we can be close to God. The Jews at one time looked down on the Gentile nation. They felt that anyone who was not a Jew was inferior to them.

But our text tells us that Christ has brought us, who were far off, nigh. "You, who once were alien's from the common wealth of Israel and strangers from the covenant of promise having no hope and without Christ in the world." But now in Christ Jesus you who were once afar off have been made near by the blood of Christ." God in Jesus Christ has broken down the middle wall of partition and brought us together. (Ephesians 2:12-14).

Often in church when the invitation to discipleship is given, many people come to the altar requesting prayer; and their prayer request is often they feel a need to be closer to God. People call into radio stations with prayer requests and one request is a desire to get closer to God. Intimacy with God ought to be a desire of all Christians.

If one desires to have closeness or intimacy with God, it requires one to enter into a covenant relationship with God. For worship to have value, the worshipper must have intimacy with God. God is both immanent and transcendent. He is near us as well as beyond us. The problem with one wanting to be close to God is not that God is far from us, but the problem lies in the fact that we remove ourselves from God. We expect God to come to us, as to say God has left us. We remove ourselves from God; He does not remove Himself from us.

Our sin or sins drive us from God. When Samson got out of the will of God the scripture says that the spirit of the Lord departed from Samson and he did not know it. We see the intimacy Adam once had with God was lost because of sin. When Adam and Eve had both sinned they hid themselves from God and lost intimacy with God. They lost the intimacy and closeness they once had with God and were moved from the presence of God.

We cannot hide nor flee from God. We may leave God but God does not leave us. God is always present. He is omnipresent, meaning He is everywhere. The psalmist says, "Where shall I flee from thy spirit or where shall I flee from thy presence, if I make my bed in hell thou art there, if I take the wings of an eagle and ascend into the uttermost part of the earth thou art there." (Psalms 139: 7-8). (*Romans 10:6-7*) says "Who shall ascend into the heavens to bring Christ down or who shall descend in the lower part of the earth to bring Christ up, but the word is nigh thee even at thy mouth, the word of faith."

Many people, many being Christians, attempt to place too much responsibility on God. It is not that God cannot handle whatever we bring to Him, God is sovereign He can do whatever He wants to do. *(Isaiah 59:1)* says, "Behold the Lord's hand is not shorten that it cannot save, nor is His ear heavy, that it cannot hear but our iniquities have separated us from God; and our sins have hidden His face from us, so that He will not hear."

God is not going to do for us those things we can do for ourselves. When God created man and made man in His image, man was given free will. We are not Tommy tons. We are free moral beings with the right to choose right from wrong provided we have been enlightened by the word of God. God has given us the right to choose our destiny. (Deuteronomy 6) says, "I have set before you life and death, blessings and cursing, good and evil; choose life."

The **first** thing we must understand about getting close to God or having intimacy with God is that getting close to God is an act of our will. God has done His part. *(James 4:8)* says, "Draw near to God and He will draw near to you." Getting close to God requires, on the part of the supplicant, to act or initiate his will. Getting close to God is an act of your will. Getting close to God is more than lip service. To say that you want to get close to God and never make an effort to get close to God is not being serious about getting close to God. The scripture says if we draw near to God He will draw near to us. The apostle Paul talked about having intimacy with God when he said, "That I might know Him and the power of His resurrection and the fellowship of His sufferings, being made conformable unto His death." The Apostle was talking about having intimacy with God by knowing Him and sharing His sufferings. One cannot know God apart from knowing Him through His sufferings. Intimacy with God calls us to enter into relationship with Him. How do we draw near to God? How do we have intimacy with God? How do we grow up in Him? We have intimacy with God when we will our will to

God.

Secondly, if we want intimacy with God we must come to God by faith. *(Hebrews 11:6)* says "But without faith it is impossible to please God, for he that would come to Him must believe that He is, and that He is a rewarder to them that diligently seek Him." The word diligent means that we earnestly, sincerely seek Him. So many people say one thing but do something else. He is a rewarder to them that diligently seek Him. *(Isaiah 55:6)* says, "Seek the Lord while He may be found, Call upon Him while He is near." How do we draw near to God? How do we seek him? Jeremiah says: if we seek Him with our whole heart we shall find Him. Intimacy with God starts with the heart. "Thou shalt love the Lord thy God with all thy heart, with all thy mind, with all thy soul, with all thy strength and thy neighbor as thyself." Our relationship with God begins with what is in our heart. God knows what is in our heart and what is in our heart will determine our relationship with God and our level of intimacy with God.

The **third thing** one must do if he or she desires intimacy with God is to seek God through studying God's word on a daily basis. To say you want to be close to God and never take time to read and study God's word does not say much about one's commitment to get close to God. *(2 Timothy 2:15)* says, "Study to show thyself approved unto God a workman needing not to be ashamed, but rightly dividing the word of truth."

If you want to be close to God you must add knowledge to your faith. The prophet Jeremiah said that the people who know their God are strong. The only way to get close to God is to know God through

His word. The word of God will become flesh and dwell in the heart of the believer.

Fourthly, we must have a passion for God if one desires to get close to God. One has to have a passion or love for God. *(Psalm 42:1-2)* says, "As the deer pants for the water brooks, so pants my soul for you, O God; My soul thirsts for God, for the loving God." To get close to God we must have a passion and a thirst for God. The gazelle tops out at about 85 mile per hour. When he sees his prey and if he does not capture his prey by the time he tops out at 85 miles per hour he will then begin to loose speed and loose heart for his prey. The reason - his heart is not that big.

This is the way it is for many Christians that say they want to be close to God. They start out zealous but soon burn out because their heart is not big enough to really want God. They lack passion of heart. They lack discipline for the things of God. Their heart is not panting for God as the deer. To get close to God one must deny his or herself of things that would come between them and God. I once talked with the legendary preacher, Dr. Gardner C. Taylor, about allowing things we know are not good for us to hinder us from getting close to God. His reply was, we have to ask ourselves a question and that question is, "What is it we allow to hinder us from getting close to God?" Do we love it more than we love God? This was the central question that Jesus asked Simon Peter, Simon do you love Me more than these? Simon's love for God would determine how dedicated he would be to the cause of Christ. Our love for God is a searching question. Getting close to God means to love God with all of our heart, mind, and soul.

Fifthly, we must exercise meditation and prayer to get close to God. Meditation is reflecting on the word of God. *(Joshua 1:8)* says, "This book of the law shall not depart out of thy mouth, but thou shall mediate on it day and night that thou may observe to be all that is written therein, then thou shall make thy way prosperous and then thou shall have good success." We must allow the word of God to speak to our hearts and minds as we meditate on the word of God.

Finally, prayer. *(Ephesians 6:18)* says, "Praying always with all prayer and supplication in the spirit, being watchful to this end with all perseverance and supplication for the saints." Men ought to always pray and faint not. Pray without ceasing. The effectual fervent prayer of the righteous avails much. The prayer of faith can save the sick. Prayer, communion with God, brings us closer to God. Prayer builds our relationship with God. Prayer strengthens our relationship with God. Prayer keeps us close to God. Prayer renews us, prayer restores us, and prayer keeps us in touch with God.

Sweet hour of prayer, sweet hour of prayer that calls me from a world of care, and bids me at My father's throne make all my wants and wishes known.

7

Is It the Devil or Is It You?

(Ephesians 6:10-18)

We often hear people say the devil made me do it or the devil got in me or I let the devil get in me. The comedian Flip Wilson used to say, "The devil made me do it." We live in a world where people are not willing to take full responsibility for their actions, especially when they are wrong. People often look for something or someone to blame for their poor choices or mistakes. To say the devil made me do it or the devil got in me, or I let the devil take over, is to say that as a Christian we give the devil too much credit or the devil has more influence and power over our lives than God does. When I hear people say the devil made me do it or the devil got in me or I let the devil take over, I wonder is it the devil or is it the person saying it is the devil.

This is a question we all need to ask ourselves when we fall short of the glory of God and fail to do what's right. If the devil can get in a person who says they are a Christian and rule that person, this says that person has more of the devil in them than they have God in them. We have seen in Luke's gospel where demons took control of a man and bound him until Jesus set him free. The bible says, "Whom the Son has set free is free indeed." The bible states that as Christians, "Greater is He, meaning God that is in us, than he, meaning the Devil that is in the world."

Now we know that we do not wrestle against flesh and blood, but against principalities, against the rulers of darkness of this world, against spiritual wickedness in high places *(Ephesians 6:12)*. This verse would have us to know that the forces of evil are against us. The word "against" is used four times in this verse. We come up against many forces of evil in life's journey as a Christian.

The Apostle Paul talks about the prince and the power of the air, the spirit that now works in the children of disobedience *(Ephesians 2:2)*. This verse tells us that when we are disobedient the spirit of darkness is at work in the children of disobedience. The devil seizes the opportunity to take advantage of the believer when the believer is disobedient to God. We see an example of this in the life of Jonah. God instructed Jonah to go Nineveh to preach and tell the people to repent. Jonah, because he had a personal vendetta toward the people disobeyed God. When Jonah disobeyed God, the spirit of the devil went to work in Jonah. When we disobey God we bring the judgment of God upon us. The devil will work in those who are disobedient. When one disobeys God in their tithing, the devil will entice you to buy things that will keep you in debt and you will never have enough money and you will not be able to tithe. The devil does not always entice us to sin, but he uses our bad habits to keep us from being obedient to God.

The devil knows the weak and vulnerable areas of our lives and those are the areas he will attack when we are disobedient to God. We see that blaming the devil just did not start; this started with Eve in the Garden of Eden. Blaming someone else for sin started in the beginning of creation. We see Eve blaming the Devil for her actions when God asked her what was it that she had done when she ate from the forbidden tree in the garden. "And the woman said, 'the serpent, meaning the devil, beguiled, tricked me, and I did eat.'" Then Adam blamed Eve for his actions and stated to God, "That woman you gave me, gave me to eat" (Genesis 3:12). Adam did not want to take responsibility for his actions, but wanted to blame Eve and God. Does the devil have that much power to make one go against God or is it just that we choose to do what we want to do and blame it on the devil? Some people have blamed God for their mistakes and actions. Is it that we are powerless and helpless over the devil or we do not have control over our own actions and we blame the devil? The question that should concern all of us is, if we can recognize when it is the devil, so we say, why can we not recognize when it is our own doing and not the devil? If you ask a person why they did not come to church or Sunday school, they will say the devil started this morning or I let the devil get in the way. If you ask them why they act ugly sometimes, they will tell you well you know we are still human and the devil knows where to attack us. It appears that some people know more about the devil than they know about themselves. Some people seem to know more about the devil than they know about God. There are some things we must know and understand about the devil and ourselves. How can we know when things come upon us if it is the devil or if it is us?

The **first thing** we must know about the devil is that he is our adversary; he is against the people of God. (1 Peter 5:8) says, "Be sober, and be vigilant;

because your adversary the devil, as a roaring lion, walketh about; seeking whom he may devour." We must know and understand that the devil opposes us because he opposed God. We must know, according to the word of God that Satan is the God of this world. His job is to deceive us, by telling us as he did Eve, that we can be something that God did not intend us to be, as well as wanting us to think that God wants to conceal truths from us. Satan deceived Eve into questioning and doubting the word of God. Satan wanted Eve to believe that if she ate from the tree of knowledge that she would be as God. We must know that if the devil was against God, then he is also against us as the people of God.

The **second thing** we learn about the devil is that he is an accuser of the brethren. (Revelations 12:10) says, "For the accuser of the brethren is cast down which accuse them before our God day and night." The devil is always accusing the believer before God. We see this having taken place in the life of Job. Satan is always propositioning God when it comes to the people of God. Satan feels that he can go to God and tell God something he thinks that God does not already know about us. Satan will try to tell God that he can have a greater influence on us than God can. Satan told God that if He would move the hedges from around Job he could make Job deny his faith. What we learn from Job was that in spite of all that had happened to him and that came against him, Job said, "I know that my redeemer lives." If we do not know that our redeemer lives, Satan will be able to prevail in our lives.

The **third thing** that we must understand about the devil is that he never gives up. He will depart for only a season. We see this also when he tempted Jesus in the wilderness. Luke's gospel tells us that when Satan ended his temptations he departed for a season. He will always regroup and return. We must understand that his mission is to destroy us as well as to get us to deny the faith. He will change his approach, he will alter his strategies but he does not give up.

The **fourth thing** we must know to discern if it's the devil or if it is us is to know that we can be the problem. We all have free will and we make choices whether they are right or wrong. Now whether we do what's right or wrong, and whether we let the devil in or not God still holds us accountable. Once we as Christians have heard the truth there is no excuse. Some of the sins or things we do are of the devil. Lying is of the devil, hate is of the devil, jealousy is of the devil, envy is of the devil, and murder is of the devil. If we do not know how to recognize the works of the devil, he will have us doing his evil works. When we get in the flesh and serve the flesh it is not the devil, it's the one who is in the flesh. (Romans 8:8) says, "They that are in the flesh cannot please God."

The **fifth thing** we must do when we know it is the devil and it is not us; is to resist the devil. Before we can resist the devil we must first submit to God. (James 4:7) says, "Submit yourselves therefore unto God, resist the devil, and he will flee from you." Resist means not to give into the devil but oppose him. Defy him with the word of God. Jesus dealt with the devil when He was in the wilderness with the word of God. The weapons of our warfare are carnal but mighty through God to the pulling down of strongholds. The only way we will ever be able to defeat the devil is by using the Word of God. For every trick the devil uses there is a word of God that can counteract the devil's approach. Jesus used His spiritual weapons to defeat the wiles of the devil.

The **sixth thing** we must do when we know it is the devil is not to give him any room to work. (Ephesians 4:27) says, "Neither give place to the devil." We cannot give him any place or anything to work with and he will have to leave. The mistake that Eve made with the serpent was to entertain him. She took up time with him. She allowed him to come in by entertaining him with an ungodly conversation. She was not aware that the serpent was exalting himself against the knowledge of God. God had set the boundaries and stated that if they went beyond the boundaries what would happen. Eve allowed the serpent to influence her, to doubt the truth about what God said about the tree of knowledge of good and evil. Satan will turn the truth into a lie if we are ignorant of the word of God. We must know how we allow the devil to come in, but he cannot come in unless we give him a place to take up residence.

The **seventh and final thing** is to put on the whole armor of God: The girdle of truth, the breastplate of righteousness, our feet shod with the preparation of the gospel of peace, the shield of faith, the helmet of salvation, the sword of the spirit which is the word of God, and praying always with prayer and supplication. (Luke 18:1) says, "Men ought to always pray and faint not." We must pray without ceasing. The spirit that knows the mind of the spirit makes intercession for us with groanings that cannot be uttered. The devil does not know what we are saying when we are praying, but the spirit knows. We must have on the helmet of salvation; we must know that we are saved, having the certainty of our salvation. Some people are not sure of their salvation. We must have the girdle of truth on us. The Roman legendary solider would wear a girdle. The girdle was used to tighten up or secure any loose ends he had hanging down. The Christian has to be secure; get a handle on any bad habits or flaws that often trip or hinder them. The girdle of truth is that we must get a handle on those flaws or bad habits and bring them into subjection. The breastplate of righteousness; we must present ourselves before the devil as the righteousness of God. The devil knows if we are pretending, if we are genuine or counterfeit. In Acts, the ninetieth chapter, there were vagabond Jews who attempted to use the name of Jesus in dealing with the evil spirits but were overtaken because they had the wrong motives. The evil spirits said, "Jesus I know, Paul I know; but who are you." The devil knows who we are and whom we belong too. We must have our feet shod with the preparation of the Gospel of peace. The Roman soldier was always prepared to wage war with the enemy. He always had his shoes on; he lived in a state of readiness at all times. As Christians we must always be prepared to face the enemy. The shield of faith; the soldier would have a shield that covered and protected him from the top of his head to the bottom of his feet. It was wide enough to protect his sides. The word of God shields us from top to bottom and covers our sides. And finally the Sword of the spirit; Jesus said, "My word is spirit and life." The word of God is a lamp unto our feet and a light unto our path. The word of God is pure; it is a shield unto them that put their trust in Him. The word of God is sharper than any two-headed sword. The word of God is forever settled in heaven. Heaven and earth shall pass away but My word, says Jesus shall abide forever.

When a Boy Has to Do a Man's Job

(1 Samuel 17:1-11)

We live in a world or society where men as a whole are in a crisis. There is a crisis of identity for most young men today regardless of their race. The crisis stems from men having no sense of their purpose and a lack of their identity. Many men fail to know their raison detre, their reason for being or their purpose. Many men, not knowing who they are, fail to understand their purpose and find themselves out of place in their family, church and community.

The role of men has changed over the years due to economics, education, and politics; this has caused a breakup and breakdown in the family. A man being able to provide and protect his family was once what defined being a man. He was once the soul provider and breadwinner of his family. Those times have changed and men are no longer the soul providers of their families. Most women today make more money than men. Although the roles of men and women have changed, historically speaking, the purpose of men has not changed. Men are being challenged more now than they have ever been. As men we are being challenged to rise up and fulfill our role and God given purpose as men.

There are different areas that help define a man. When we seek to define a man we have to define a man from six different perspectives. Spirituality, morality, personality, sexuality, intellectuality, and practicality all help define a man. The Marines some years ago coined a slogan, "Looking for a few good Men." In our churches today women outnumber men. Young woman today say they are looking for men who have been born again. They are looking for men to protect them, be their spiritual leader and guide. They are looking for men to provide emotional strength and moral support. Men are being called upon to provide emotional strength more so than financial support for women. But what we find in today's society is that most men are out of place or do not know or understand their purpose as it relates to their family. The prison systems are running over with men of all races.

Some minority groups outnumber others in the system. Statistics show that eighty to ninety percent of all black males before going to prison have never been to church. Something is wrong with this picture. In our text we see the nation of Israel being challenged by the armies of the Philistines. Saul was the king of Israel and the philistines were being led by a great and mighty warrior name Goliath. Goliath issues a challenge to the men of Israel to step up and respond to his challenge. Goliath stood and shouted, "Give me a man that we may fight together." They were to fight and decide who would serve the other. There are giants in the world that we as men have to face every day in our lives. The giant of racism and discrimination shows its face in the job market, in political arenas and other social disciplines in the world. It will show its face in the church if we are not careful. When Goliath stood up and issued his challenge to Israel there was no man to be found who would answer the call. The text says when Saul and the armies heard these words they were dismayed and so afraid. There was not a man to be found that would step up to the challenge.

What often happens when men will not step up and fulfill their God given purpose and role is that, women will have to assume the role of both the mother and the father. When a job needs to be done God will use whoever will step up. When I was a young boy growing up, my father and mother were separated due to their irreconcilable differences. There were eight boys my mother had to raise in the absentia of my father. There were many days I had to step up at the age of eight or nine and go out into the community and rake leaves and mow neighbor's lawns to earn money to help my mother provide food and other staples for my seven brothers. Here we have David, the son of Jesse, a young boy stepping up to do a man's job. We hear David asking the question, "Who is this uncircumcised philistine who defies the armies of the living God, Is there not a cause?" Here was a boy stepping up to do a man's job because Saul and his men were afraid to step up and respond to the challenge issued by Goliath. We need men who will see a cause and be willing to step up and fight for that cause. We need men who will see a need and cause to volunteer sometimes to be mentors for young males who are at risk. We need men who have sons who will not only tell their sons to be a man but show them how to be a man.

I have served in many capacities where I have been around men of all ages. Once I served as an intervention specialist/counselor at a middle school, and there was young male student named Sammy.

Sammy came from a home where there was no male figure or role model in his home. Sammy's father was in prison and Sammy's mother was a drug addict and he and his older brother were living with their grandmother who had health concerns. The principal and teachers felt that Sammy was basically a good kid but needed some guidance and structure in his life. They were concerned about Sammy and wanted him to succeed. They told me that they felt I was a good role model for Sammy. I asked Sammy one day if he felt I was too hard on him and he stated no, but stated that he realized that I was only trying to help him do what was in his best interest. I asked Sammy on the last day I would be working with him what he learned from me and what would he remember most about me. He stated that he realized that I cared about him and that I had been a good role model for him. I was deeply moved by his reply. "If I can help somebody as I travel along, if I can show somebody that they are going wrong, if I can cheer somebody with a word or a song, then my living will not be in vain."

But what is man? The scriptures say in (*Psalms 8* and *Hebrews 2:6-8*), "What is man that thou art mindful of him, or the son of man that thou considers him, thou has made him a little lower than the angels and crowned him with glory and honor and set him over the work of thy hands and have put all things under his feet." How do we measure a man and what helps to define a man?

The **first thing** we do to measure a man is to first look at his relationship with God. Martin Luther King, Jr. said in his book, "The Measure of a Man," that a man is measured first by his vertical relationship with God. How he reaches up to God. Most men today do not have a relationship with God. Many attend church but there is no relationship with God that brings about intimacy with God. Men must have a relationship with God so they will have intimacy with God.

I once talked with a young man who was experiencing family problems. As we talked about family and other things that were important in life as it related to men and their roles in their families, he went on to talk about his grandfather. He stated that he remembered growing up watching his grandfather. He said that his grandfather was a very happy and peaceful man. He stated that his grandfather did not have a formal education but he always appeared to be happy. He would watch his grandfather sing a verse of a song and pray before he went to bed each evening. He went on to say that he had an education and a good paying job but he was never at peace. He said that he had lost his family because he valued his career more than his family. Then one day he asked himself, what was it that his grandfather had he did not have. His grandfather never had an education but he was a happy and peaceful man. He had an education and money but he felt empty. He stated that what he concluded was that his grandfather had spirituality and that was what he was lacking.

The **second thing** that measures a man is how he sees himself as being made in the image of God. A man's self image is measured by the God in him. Our self worth comes from our understanding of who God is. We must value ourselves because God created us in His image and in His likeness. Man must realize that God has set His affection upon him. As men, we must have a sense of who we are, who we belong to, as well as whom we are serving and believe that things with man are impossible but with God all things are possible to them that believe. We must realize we are nothing apart from God. Our worth and value evolves from our sense of who we are in Jesus Christ. We are a royal priesthood, a peculiar people. We must realize that God has given to each of us authority and has set us over the works of His hands, and that we have been created in Christ Jesus for good works.

The **third and final** thing we want to look at that measure and defines a man is the horizontal. What I mean by the horizontal is how he reaches out to his neighbor. "Thou shall Love the Lord thy God and thy neighbor as thyself." As men we must love the brethren, "For we know that we have passed from death unto life because we love the brethren." There is too much black on black crime. I once eulogized a twenty-eight year old black male who had been killed in his home. Weeks after his death the father of this young man and I were talking about his son and he stated to me, "Pastor its hard to tell young men about eternal life when they don't value human life." We need men that will step up and say to our young men that life is sacred and that we must learn to value one another and in valuing one another we then respect the God in each of us. Only God can give human life but anyone can take it away. We need men who will step up and teach our young men that life is a gift. We need men who will step up and teach our young men to value our young women. Jesus told His disciples to "love one another as I have loved you."

Give me a man who will step up like Martin Luther King, Jr., and lead the civil rights movement to bring equality and justice to all people.

Give me a man like Joseph who was willing to step up and be a man of morals and values and not sleep with his master's wife.

Give me a man like Moses who was willing to suffer for the things of God than to enjoy the pleasures of this life for a season.

Give me a man like Daniel who was willing to step up to the king and not bow down and serve a god that was an idol.

Give me a man like John the Baptist who was willing to step up to King Herod and tell him he was living in sin.

Give me a man like Moses who was willing to lead a freedom march for the children of Israel.

Give me a man like David, although he was a shepherd boy, who was willing to step up and fight the giant Goliath.

Give me a man like the Apostle John who was banished to the Isle of Patmos because he was willing to step up and not bow down to Dominican and call him Lord.

Give me a man like Jesus who was willing to disrobe Himself and lay aside His royal diadem and get into the chariot of time and come into this low land of sorrow and redeem a dying world.

Rise up, o men of God have done with lesser things. Give heart and mind and soul and strength to serve the King of Kings. If men would rise up we could take our streets back.

If men would rise up we could raise young boys to be better men. If men would rise up and fulfill their role as men then there would be less young men behind prison walls.

If men would rise up then our young women

would have decent young men to marry.

If men would rise up as David rose up, they would experience and know that when we stand for a cause, we do not stand alone, we stand in the power of His might. When we feel insufficient we become sufficient when we commit what we have to God.

If men would rise up, heaven would come down our souls to greet and glory would crown the mercy seat.

9

No Other Name for Salvation

(Matthew 1:18-25, Acts 4:1-12)

We live in a day and time when the Christian religion is under attack. The issue of prayer in school has always been an issue. They say prayer in school violates the constitution as it relates to the separation of church and state, or it's offensive to those who are non-Christians. I was in a chaplain's commission conference once and one of the issues that were a topic of discussion was religious pluralism and the protection of civil liberties that were challenging military chaplains in their ministry. One of the challenges for evangelical protestant chaplains was being able to pray in the name of Jesus. Some commanders and senior chaplains had requested and demanded that chaplains refrain from praying in the name of Jesus in their public prayers. The problem now is not praying but the name that's being referred to when one prays.

There is a religious group that is seeking a civil religion. A civil religion is a religion that excludes certain religious language. Christianity is the only religion where other religions are offended in public settings when the name of Jesus is used. The United States Supreme Court has issued rulings that government bodies may agree only to generic prayers. What this means is that as long as prayers do not have the name of Jesus then they are permitted. But prayers that use the name of Jesus are not condoned.

The objection to praying in Jesus' name is that non-Christians feel excluded. They want chaplains to pray non-sectarian prayers, prayers that exclude the name of Jesus. The irony here is that these exclusive claims are not leveled against a Rabbi, who offers prayers in Hebrew or the Inman, or who is Arabic who recites from the Koran and prays to Allah. These prayers of other religions are sectarian, and no one has a problem but when the name of Jesus is used then other religions are offended and object. Our text tells us His name shall be called Jesus, for He shall save His people from their sins.

What we see happening regarding the use of the name of Jesus is that Christians are being asked not to acknowledge the name of Jesus publicly. Jesus said, "Whoever confesses Me before men, him will I also confess before My Father who is in heaven." As Christians we must not forget our identity with Jesus Christ. Because of Jesus we are citizens of the kingdom of heaven. Jesus warned His disciples before He departed that they would be hated for his namesake. "Blessed are you when men shall revile you, and persecute you, and shall say all manner of evil against you falsely, for my sake." (Matthew 5:11). Jesus warned His disciples that they could not avoid being hated for His name's sake.

The name of Jesus has always offended people. Every name has significance. When the prophet Isaiah prophesied about the coming of Jesus he did not state His name. He said, "He shall be called Wonderful, Counselor, the mighty God, the everlasting Father, and the Prince of Peace." (Isaiah 9:6) But in Luke's gospel account he states that His name shall be called Jesus, for He shall save His people from their sin. (Luke 1: 31). Luke tells us that salvation would come through and in the name of Jesus. Jesus told His disciples that if they would ask anything in His name it would be given. Those who have been offended are people of other religious groups. The Apostle John who revealed and wrote the book of Revelation was banished to the Isle of Patmos because he refused to say Dominican was lord, but Jesus was Lord.

The Reverend Franklin Graham, spoke and prayed at Columbine High School and President Bush's inauguration, was ridiculed by other religious groups for lifting up the name of Jesus. Pastor Kirbyjon Caldwell of Houston Texas was also chided for using the name of Jesus when he gave the prayer of benediction at President Bush's Inauguration. The young high school student at Columbine High school lost her life because she confessed faith in Jesus Christ. She was willing to die for her faith and the name of Jesus.

The name of Jesus has always been under attack. We live in a country where the name of Jesus offends others who are not Christians. Our country is more tolerant with other religious groups and their beliefs than it is with Christianity. But the Apostle Peter says, "There is no other name whereby men must be saved but the name of Jesus." When the name of Jesus is used in a religious arena or school someone is always offended. But, "There is no other name whereby men must be saved."

After September 11th, the California school district required the seventh grade students to learn the tenets of Islam and to learn verses from the Koran.

They were to pray in the name of ALLAH the lord of creation. Now if Christianity had been a requirement in the school system there would have been a lawsuit saying it was a violation of the separation of the church and the state. "There is no other name whereby men must be saved but the name of Jesus." In the prayer the students had to say that Allah is Lord of creation.

The scriptures say, "the name of the Lord is a strong and mighty tower, the righteous run unto it and are safe." (Proverbs 18:10). Jesus is not only the Son of God; He is God in the person of Jesus Christ, His Son. He is not only the Lord of creation; He is the Lord of lords, kings of kings, and the God of all Gods. He is not only Creator but He is Savior and Lord. He is not only Savior but also Redeemer, not only Redeemer, but also Comforter, not only Comforter but also keeper of our soul. So there is no other name whereby men must be saved. Jesus warned His disciples that they would be hated for His namesake. What is the relationship between salvation and the name of Jesus?

The **first thing** we need to know about this name is that eternal life comes only through the name of Jesus. Jesus told the woman at Jacob's well if she knew the gift of God and who was asking her for a drink of water, she would ask Him to give her the living water. *(Romans 6:23)* says, "For the wages of sin is death but the gift of God is eternal life." Jesus offered the woman at the well eternal life. Salvation only comes in the name of Jesus. *(St. John 1:12)* says, "For as many as received Him, to them He gave the right to become the children of God, to those who believe on His name."

The **second thing** we need to know about the name of Jesus is that if we want to come to God we have to get there through Jesus. Jesus said in *(John 14:6),* "I am the way, the truth and the life, no man cometh to the Father, but by Me." Jesus is our way out, our way through, and our way in. *(2Corinthians 5:19)* says, "Now God was in Christ reconciling the world unto Himself, not imputing their trespasses unto them; and hath committed unto us the word reconciliation." To reconcile means to befriend, bring back into relationship. There is only one mediator between God and man, the man Christ Jesus. He intercedes for us and He is our intercessor. He is our great high priest who has entered into the Holy of Holies on our behalf. He takes our case before God the Father. He pleads our case before God the Father. He is touched with the feelings of our infirmities and weaknesses. He was tempted as we are yet without sin. He is our only way to God. God sees us through Jesus.

When we stand before God the Father and come into our inheritance, and we are asked for our title and we have not paid our bill in full, Jesus will say let him in because he is with me. I have paid the price and purchased his salvation in My Own blood.

The **third thing** we need to know about His name, is that there is authority in His name. A Christian has neither power nor authority to do the work of the church without the authority of His name. Jesus said in *(Matthew 7: 21-23),* "That many will use His name without His authority. Many will say to Me in that day, Lord we have prophesied in your name, cast out demons in your name, and done many wonders in your name. And then I will declare to them, I never knew you: depart from Me you who practice lawlessness." When we do not have the authority to use His name our works are of no avail. To have the authority to use His name we have to be Christians. Being a Christian says God has given us the authority and empowered us to use His name. In our text when Peter was asked by what authority or name the lame man was healed, He stated, "Let it be known to all, that by the name of Jesus Christ of Nazareth whom you crucified, whom God raised from the dead, by Him this man stands here before you whole."

The **fourth thing** we must know about this name is that this name brings a reward to them who believe and call on His name. *(John 3:16)* says, "For God so loved the world that He gave His only begotten Son that whoever believes in Him shall not perish but have everlasting life." *(Romans 10:13)* says, "For whosoever calls upon the name of the Lord shall be saved." If you want to be saved, confess the name of Jesus and call on His name. For with the heart, man believes unto righteousness and with the mouth confession is made unto salvation. For there is no other Name whereby men must be saved, but the name of Jesus.

The **fifth thing** we need to know about His name is the security we have in His name. As Christians we have eternal security because of the name of Jesus. It does not matter what is happening around us; we are secure in Him. Jesus said, "And I give unto them eternal life; and they shall never perish, neither shall any man pluck them out of My hand. My Father, which gave them to Me, is greater than all; and no man is able to pluck them out of My Father's hand. I and My Father are one." (John 10: 28-30). We have security that comes through both the Father and the Son. In (Psalm 91: 14), the Lord says to David, "Because he has set his affection upon Me, therefore will I deliver him; I will set him on high because he has known My name." There is security in knowing His name. There are benefits in knowing His Name. There is deliverance in knowing His Name.

The **sixth and final thing** we know about His name is that all men will bow at the name of Jesus. *(Philippians 2:10)* says, "That at the name of Jesus every knee should bow of those in heaven and those on earth, and that every tongue shall confess that Jesus Christ is Lord, to the glory of God the Father." The white knee shall bow to the name of Jesus. The black knee shall bow to the name of Jesus. The brown knee shall bow to the name of Jesus. The rich knee, the poor knee, the fat knee, the skinny knee, every knee shall bow to the name of Jesus.

The story is told that a few weeks in the aftermath of 9-11, Franklin Graham, president of Samaritan's Purse which deals with international relief, went to New York to set up prayer lines for families to call in for prayer but the power lines were out due to the 9-11 explosion. Franklin Graham sent a team to the telephone company and requested that the telephone lines be restored so they could set up prayer lines. Well they were told that it would take about four weeks before they would be able to restore the telephone lines in that area. Well the representative Franklin Graham had sent came back and reported to Franklin what the telephone company said - that it would take four weeks for them to restore power to the telephone lines. Franklin sent the representative back and told him to tell them that Franklin Graham, the son of Billy Graham, sent him. When the man at the telephone company heard that it was Billy Graham's son his reply to the man was to tell Franklin Graham that they would have the telephone lines set up in two or three days. The name of Billy Graham had power and influence. I may not be able use Billy Graham's name but I know a name.

I know a name that can call the prodigal home. I know a name that can cleanse the leper's spots. I know a name that can make the wounded whole. I know a name that can set the captive free. I know a name that's all together lovely. I know a name that can speak and men live. I know a name that can speak and men die. I know a name that saves to the uttermost. I know a name Jehovah-jireh my provider, I know a name Jehovah-nissi the lord my banner, I know a name Jehovah-shalom the Lord is my peace. I know a name Jehovah-shammah, the Lord is there, I know a name Jehovah—tsebaoth, the Lord of hosts, I know a name Jehovah-Elohe Israel, the Lord God of Israel. I know a name that saves to the uttermost, that name is Jesus.

10

Biblical Principles for Nurturing Our Children

(Deuteronomy 6:4-7)

Often we hear the maxim, "That our children are our future." When we look at the future of our children and how they are being raised and the circumstances in which many are being raised we have to wonder, do they have a future? Many children today are subjected to many immoral things in life in their families. Many are being misguided and taught the wrong things by what they see their parents do. To say that children are our future and not provide a safe nurturing environment for them to grow up in robs them of any possible future. Many children are growing up in families today where they are abused emotionally, physically, sexually and mentally; leaving them damaged. Some of these effects are irreversible. When these social pathologies are happening to our children, it makes it difficult for them to have a future. Their pain and issues will have to first be addressed if they are to possibly have a future.

There are many whose futures have been taken from them at a very early age. There is an avalanche of ideas that are given by psychologists and sociologists regarding how children should be developed and nurtured. The relationship between parents and children has degenerated over the years due to a number of factors. The break down in the family, where there are many single parents. Many men who have fathered children are in prison or out of place and fail to spend quality time with the family or the child. Many children today grow up with feelings of alienation, animosity, frustration, anger, and rebellion. Throughout the country there is an alarming rise in teenage alcoholism and drug abuse. There is an alarming rise in premarital sex among teenagers. Children looking for love from their parents that they never get so they seek love and a sense of belonging in other places that are the wrongs places. There is an African proverb that says, "It takes a village to raise a child." The village has been dissolved and for most young teenage males, gangs have replaced the village. I was told by a new teenager that a gang was his family.

Psychologists, sociologists and teachers have influenced parents to believe that disciplining a child is too restrictive or extreme. This has led to a generation of young people who have no respect for authority. This began in homes where parents have been more incline to believe ungodly teachers and psychologists than the word of God. Due to a lack of discipline in the home, which has led to a lack of respect for authority, it has been said that many teachers fear for their lives and safety in the classroom. What can we do to better nurture and prepare our children in order that they can have a promising future as well as be our future? What can parents do to better equip their children for the future?

The **first biblical principle** that parents need to teach their children that will make things better for their children is to demonstrate a spiritual oneness between each other. A marriage will never be what God has intended it to be unless it is based on the principles God has given for the marriage. Many families lack spiritual oneness, or unity within the family unit. God has designed marriage to be a oneness of mind, oneness of emotions, oneness of the body and oneness of the spirit. If there is no unity in these areas of a marriage the whole family is affected. Families need to worship together, pray together and serve one another in the spirit of unity and the bond of peace. When children see their parents on one accord it gives them stability as well a sense of belonging. I have counseled many young teenagers who suffered with attachment disorder. What I mean is that many have lived with a number of different families due to the fact they have come from families that did not afford them a stable and safe living environment. They lack a sense of belonging, therefore, becoming attached to a number of different families becomes difficult for them each time they are placed with a different family due to their behavior.

Parents have to demonstrate love to one another around their children emotionally, physically, mentally and spiritually. The husband has to be sensitive to the needs of the wife and the wife has to be sensitive to the needs of the husband. The parents must cleave together, meaning stick together. Two people that love each other must be sensitive and affectionate toward one another. Some children never see their parents touch one another. Psychologists and physicians say the power of the touch heals not only the body but also the soul. Touching a person calms their fears, lessens pain, and alleviates discouragement. A young girl told her father one day that she knew that he did not love her and the father replied what makes you feel that I don't love you. The young girl's reply to her father was, "Father you never touch me or hug me." The bible teaches us that we are to love not only in word but in deed.

The **second biblical principle** we are to teach our children is to start teaching and training them at an early age. *(Proverbs 19:18)* says "Chasten the child before it is too late." To chasten means to correct and discipline at an early age. Our text, *(Deuteronomy 6:6-7)* says, "Thou shall teach them." What arc we to teach our children? We are to teach them spiritual and moral values based on the word of God. Parents must learn the word of God so they will be able to teach the word and the commands of God to their children. When a child is rebellious, the parents should teach that according to the word of God, rebellion is witchcraft, an abomination in the sight of God *(1 Samuel 15:23)*. *(Isaiah 30:1)* says, "Woe unto the rebellious child." When rebellion is stopped first in the home then there will be no rebellion outside the home. If parents teach their children rebellion and a lack of respect for authority, then the child will grow up being rebellious and not respectful to authority. If parents are passive and condone their children's behavior what happens is what happened to Eli and his children; they were all brought to destruction *(1 Samuel 2:12-36)*. If parents are rebellious, then they will produce rebellious children. Rebellion begets rebellion, what one sows is what one reaps.

The **third biblical principle** we are to teach our children is obedience. *(Ephesians 6:1)* says, "Children obey your parents in the Lord for this is right." Parent's best teach their children obedience by being obedient to the word of God themselves. It is wrong to tell a child to do as I say do and not as I do. God has promised that He would bless an obedient child. The scripture says to the obedient child that it will be well with thee. Obedience brings the blessings of God. The spiritual principle of obedience teaches us that God will reward our lives. A lady in our church talked about her grandmother who nurtured her. She said that her grandmother told her when she was growing up that if she would give her eighteen years of obedience that God would bless her life and a way would be made for her when she became a grown woman. She said that her grandmother taught her obedience and she discovered that everything her grandmother taught, regarding being obedient, was true. When she became a woman, God rewarded her life immensely. She went on to say that because she was obedient many of the mistakes many young people make in life she did not have to experience or go through. "Thou shalt teach them."

The fourth and final biblical principle we are to teach our children, as we develop them, is to honor and love God. Our text says, "Hear O Israel: the Lord thy God is one Lord. And thou shall love the Lord thy God with all thine heart, with all thine soul, with all thy might. And these words, which I command you this day, shall be in thine heart: and thou shalt teach them diligently to thy children, and thou shall talk of them when thou sittest down in thine house, and when thou walkest by the way. And when thou liest down and when thou risest up." (Deuteronomy 6:4-7). There are parents who are teaching their children to love things instead of loving God and one another. There are parents who are guilty of thinking that giving their children things means that they love them. We teach our children to love God by showing them God's love. As parents we cannot tell our children to love God when we portray the love of God to them in such way that will turn them from God when they are older. The only God many of our children will ever see is the God that should live in each of us. We must teach our children that loving God means that they are to love their neighbors as themselves. Loving God means that the things that we do to one another are things done unto God. We must teach them that, "eye has not seen, ear has not heard, neither has it entered into the heart of man the things that God has prepared for them that love Him." (1Corinthians 2:9) We must teach our children that, "God so loved the world that He gave His only begotten Son that whosoever believes in Him shall not perish but have eternal life." (John 3:16)

We must teach our children that there abideth three faith, hope and love, but the greatest of these is love. Love suffers long, and is kind. Love does not envy; love does not parade itself, is not puffed up. Love does not behave rudely, does not seek its own, is not provoked, thinks no evil; does not rejoice in iniquity, but rejoices in the truth; bears all things, believes all things, hopes all things, endures all things. Love never fails.

11

Saved To Serve

(Romans 15: 1-17)

When one becomes a Christian so often they believe that confessing faith in Jesus Christ is all that is required of them. Many feel that as long as they come to church they are all right. When God calls us to salvation, He also calls us into service. God calls us out of darkness into His marvelous light of grace. Living for God requires being of service for God. When a person joins a church he or she must feel called to that church's ministry. When a person joins a church they are called to share in the mission and vision God has given the pastor for that church. Many professing Christians feel that as long as they attend church on a regular basis and pay their tithes, they are all right. Service always follows salvation and conversion. When Isaiah was saved in the year King Uzziah died, and when the triune Godhead issued the call, "Who will go for Us," Isaiah responded, "Here am I send me." Isaiah had a readiness to go forth and serve. Every Christian should have a readiness to serve God. God has not called us to salvation for us to be idle. When God saves us, He saves us to serve. Many people who consider themselves to be Christians feel all that is required of them is to come to church and sit. I once had a man tell me that he did not want to do anything in church but come sit and worship.

If one has truly been saved then one must understand that they are called to serve. When a person becomes a Christian, he or she has been called into the ministry. Being called into ministry does not necessary mean one has been called to preach or teach or to evangelize, but one has been called to serve. The word minister in our text means service. There are many ways in which a person can serve in a ministry other than preaching or teaching. There is no such thing as an inactive church member, other than the person being physically, mentally and or emotionally incapacitated and they are unable to serve in a viable way. Every person who says he or she is saved should desire to be used by God in a fruitful and productive way. We are called to build up the body of Christ, not to tear it down. There is no room in the kingdom of God or the body of Christ for unfruitfulness or purposeless. Whether you are active or inactive you are working with God or against God. God has called us to ministry to minister through us. There are numerous areas in which we can minister besides preaching or teaching.

God does not save us to waste us. God has a plan for us even before He saves us. The prophet Jeremiah states in 29:11, "I know the plans I have for you, saith the Lord, plans of peace, and not of evil, to give you an expected end." The Apostle Paul states that we are laborers together with God, in (1 Corinthians 3:9). When we are saved we become a part of God's network. Paul says in (Ephesians 2:10), "For we are His workmanship, created in Christ Jesus unto good works, which God hath before ordained that we should walk in them."

The fiftieth chapter of Romans focuses on ministry

and service. There are six ministries in which we are called to exercise our gifts.

The **first ministry** we are called to minister is the ministry of **encouragement**. (Romans 15: 2) says, "Let every one of us please his neighbor for his good to edification." Edification comes from the word edifice, meaning building. Edification means to build up. We build one another up by encouraging one another. Some people, who are Christians (so they say) always have something negative to say. They are not doing anything and they try to discourage others for what they are doing for the kingdom of God or the body of Christ. Some people believe they are called to the ministry of discouragement. They spend more time being negative and trying to tear people down than they do building others up. They are down and they want to pull others down. The only way to help someone is to build them up through encouragement. We build up others in the body of Christ by praying for them, praising them, being kind to them, and saying those things that will build them up; that they might grow up in Christ.

The **second ministry** we are called to do is the ministry of **evangelism**. We are to be about winning souls for Jesus Christ. The Bible says in (Proverbs 11:30), "He that wins souls is wise." It does not matter how beautifully you can sing, it does not matter how eloquent you can teach, it does not matter how liberally one gives, and it does not matter how circumspectly you walk. If you are not winning souls for Jesus Christ we are not operating in the ministry of evangelism. We have been called to lead and win others to Jesus Christ. It is sad to live all of your life and have never won anyone to Jesus Christ. God is not concerned about His people building great buildings and establishing programs if we are not winning souls for the kingdom of God. If we are to win others to Christ, we must, in the words of the Apostle Paul, be all things to all people. The story is told about a man involved in a rescue mission while serving on a ship one night. He had to rescue many who had to abandon another ship. He was in and out of the water. Each time he would dive into the water and rescue someone he would say, "Did I do my best, did I forget anyone?" This is the spirit of evangelism. We should want to rescue or save anyone that is sinking or lost. Our spiritual gifts matter; if we are not winning souls for Jesus Christ we are not serving the kingdom of God. Everyone who is saved should want his or her family saved. We should be about winning our loved ones souls for Christ. The Apostle Paul said, "I become all things to all men that I may win some." He did not say that he could win all men, some men was his goal.

The **third ministry is giving**. In our text, verse twenty-five and twenty-six, we read these words, "But now I go to Jerusalem to minister unto the saints. For it pleased them of Macedonia and Achaia to make a certain contribution for the poor saints which are at Jerusalem." Some people look so niggardly upon the church, meaning they are not generous to the church. It's all about what the church can to for them. They don't want to give of their time, talents, or tithes. They want to be blessed by the church but they fail to be a blessing to the church. Many people that become members of the church want the benefits of the church but do not want to give back to the church. Some don't want to give if they can't control where the funds are going or being spent. The ministry of giving allows the church to carry out the mission and vision of the church. God loves a cheerful giver. Service to God requires us to give because we are debtors. We are debtors to God; we are debtors to the Apostles. How can anyone come to church and fail to pay his or her tithes, which belong to God. When we fail to give back to God what we owe Him we become robbers of the rich blessings God has stored up for each of us. The ministry of giving makes provisions in God's house, to meet the needs of the least of these. When we give, God has promised that He would open the windows of heaven and pour out a blessing that there would not be room enough to receive. God will bless us not only financially but mentally, physically, spiritually and emotionally. Being blessed with good health means more that money; if we have our health and strength we are able to work, to think and produce.

The **fourth ministry** we are called to minister is in **fellowship**. Fellowship is one of the biblical principles the New Testament church was built on. Fellowship comes from the Greek word "Koinonia", which means to have things in common. Fellowship brings the people of God together because we have things in common. We share in the fellowship of Christ's sufferings. It's not all about you or me, we are called to share one another burdens. When a person is truly saved he or she will miss the fellowship of the body of Christ when they are absent from the body. If you do not miss the fellowship of the saints then something is wrong with your salvation. Fellowship involves being hospitable and kind to one another. Fellowship involves loving one another and serving one another. The fellowship of kindred hearts is like to that above.

The **fifth ministry** we are to serve is **prayer**. The Apostle Paul states in *(Romans 15:30),* "Now I beseech you, brethren, for the Lord Jesus Christ's sake and for the love of the spirit, that you strive together with me in yours prayers to God for me; that I may be delivered from them that do not believe in Judea; and that my service which I have for Jerusalem may be accepted of the saints." Prayer is a ministry. Prayer is not getting ready for service, it is a service. Many people in the church want the pastor to do all of the praying. The church needs to pray for the pastor at all times. Pray ye one for another. Men ought to always pray and faint not. The church needs real saints praying at all times. Prayer is a spiritual discipline. Prayer is a ministry we should exercise daily. The great evangelist Charles Finney once stated that faith moves men but prayer moves God. (Philippians 4:6) says, "But everything by prayer and supplication, with thanksgiving let your request be made known unto God, and the God of peace that passes all understanding shall keep your hearts and minds through Christ Jesus." Prayer is the soul's sincere desire. "The eyes of the Lord are upon the righteous, and His ears are open unto their prayers, but the face of the Lord is against them that do evil." (1 Peter 3:12) says, "The effectual fervent prayer of the righteous avails much." Every church needs an intercessory prayer team. Prayer is praise and thanksgiving; sometimes all we need to do is thank God for what He has already done. Prayer is intercession; I pray for you and you pray for me that whatever we are going through God will meet us at our point of need. Prayer is petition; we have to make known our request and needs to God. Prayer is supplication; sometimes we have to plead with God - pour out our souls to God earnestly and sincerely.

The **sixth and final ministry** we are called to minister in is **worship**. The word "worship" comes from the Anglo Saxon word meaning to ascribe worth and value to God. Worship means to give to the giver. The church needs worshippers today; people who will worship Him in spirit and in truth. God wants His people to come and worship Him. Come before His presence with singing. Enter into His gates with thanksgiving and into His courts with praise. Be thankful unto Him and bless His name, for the Lord is good and His mercy is everlasting. We need to bow down before Him and cry Holy, Holy, Holy, Holy, Lord God almighty. We were created to worship Him. We praise Him for what He has done, but we worship Him because of who He is. He is Jehovah Jireh, our provider; Jehovah Nissi, our Battle Fighter; Jehovah Shalom, Giver of peace; Jehovah-Rophe, our Healer; Jehovah-Shammah, the ever-present One; Jehovah-Rohi, the good Shepard. We are to worship the Lord in the beauty of holiness and in the holiness of His beauty. Worship is a way of life and we are to worship God each and everyday of our lives. We worship Him because He is God; there is none other. We worship Him because He saves to the uttermost. We worship Him because His name is above every name. We worship Him because He lives and reigns forever.

12

Seven Kingdom Principles to Live by Each New Year

(Psalm 119:97-105)

"Putting First Things First"

Throughout the bible we read and find that God is a God of principles and precepts. God has given us spiritual principles and precepts to govern our lives. Our lives are blessed when we follow God's spiritual principles and precepts. God's principles and precepts do not make us righteous or holy, only God can make us righteous and holy. However, God's principles and precepts teach us what God wills for us, what He commands of us and what He provides for us. There are some blessings God will only grant provided we follow certain principles and precepts He commands us to follow. God will not compromise or go back on His word. God's principles and precepts serve to teach us God's truth. His principles and precepts guide us into all truth. "Ye shall know the truth and the truth shall set you free." There are certain principles that God would have us to make a priority in our lives. Otherwise, our lives will never be fulfilled. All too often we put everything and everybody before God. But one of the Ten Commandments is, "Thou shalt have no other God before Me. For I am a jealous God," says the Lord.

Each New Year brings new opportunities and possibilities for each of us to amend our ways. There are Seven Kingdom principles we want to suggest, to make a priority for the New Year.

The **first Kingdom principle** we want to consider is to **seek first the Kingdom of God**. *(Matthew 6:33)* says, "Seek ye first the kingdom of God and all of His righteousness and all these things shall be added unto you." If we are going to be successful as individuals and as a church we must seek first the kingdom of God. God wants His kingdom and the work of the kingdom to be a priority in our lives. To seek God means that we are to be in pursuit of the things of God. Many people say that they want to be closer to God but they fail to seek God, pursue God on a continuous basis. (Proverbs 8:17) says, "I love them that love Me and those that seek Me early find Me." God wants to be preeminent in the lives of His people. The promise is that if we seek first the kingdom of God and His righteousness all those things that we put before God will be added unto us. God has an order that He intends for us to follow. Everything we have need of God will provide and supply if we seek first the kingdom of God. Everything we need is in the kingdom, that's why we are to seek first the kingdom of God. Health is in the kingdom, wealth is in the kingdom, salvation is in the kingdom and prosperity is in the kingdom of God. When we seek first the kingdom of God and all of His righteousness it's the father's good pleasure to give us the keys of the kingdom. When we make Him the Lord of our lives He takes control of our lives.

The **second kingdom principle** we want to follow is to **give God our first fruits**. *(Proverbs 3:9-*

10) says, "Honor the Lord with the first fruits of thine increase: So shall thy barns be filled with plenty, and thy presses shall burst out with new wine." So often we give God what's left over of our first fruits. But we are commanded to give God first from the fruits of our increase. When we give God first what belongs to Him our needs will not go unmet. Giving to God is an act of faith and obedience. "Give and it shall be given unto you; good measure, pressed down, and shaken together, and running over, shall men give into your bosom." *(Luke 6:38)* When we honor God with our first fruits, God will bless us to meet people who are in a position to bless us. God will give us favor with men who will pour into our bosom. The Apostle Paul says, "My God shall supply all your needs according to His riches in glory" (Philippians 4:19). God knows what things we have need of before we ask Him. Giving our first fruits to God shows that we are in covenant relationship with Him. (Deuteronomy 8:18) says, "But thou shalt remember the Lord thy God: for it is he that giveth thee the power to get wealth, that he may establish His covenant which he swore unto thy father, as it is this day." God is a covenant making God, and a covenant keeping God. God will not retract his word. His word is forever settled in heaven.

The **third kingdom principle** we want to follow is to **always count the cost** of the things we want to do. So often we make rash decisions and jump right into things not knowing if we will have what it takes to finish what we start. *(Luke 14:28)* tells us that, "What man, intending to build a tower, sits not down first, and counts the cost; whether he has sufficient materials to finish what he starts." Many people lack commitment, dedication, discipline and a good work ethic. There are many people who start projects but never finish what they start. Many people join the church but are not committed to church membership. We must first always count the cost. Jesus said, "If any man would come after Me let him deny himself and take of the cross and follow Me." In Dietrich Bonhofner's book, *"The Cost of Discipleship,"* it says, "When God calls a man to follow Him, He expects him to literally die." If we want to follow Christ we must count the cost. Jesus paid it all, all to Him I owe.

The **fourth kingdom principle** we want to implement is we must **choose life**. Jesus said in *(John 10:10),* "The thief comes to kill, to steal and to destroy but I am come that you might have life and have it more abundantly." We need to choose those things in life that will add quality to our lives. Life more abundantly does not mean that you get into debt over your head and beyond your means. The world presents us with many appearances of success that mislead us. *(Deuteronomy 30:19)* says, "That I have set before you this day life and death, both blessing and cursing: therefore choose life; that both you and your seed may live." God's favor is in life. Choosing life means that we must make wise decisions regarding being good stewards of our health, our material possessions, such as our finances, our educational decisions as well as our moral and spiritual decisions. Jesus said that He has come to give us life and live more abundantly. The abundant life involves having sufficient income, healthcare, education, appropriate housing and justice for all. We are not to walk in the counsel of the ungodly nor sit in the seat of the scornful. Our delight should be in the law of the Lord.

The **fifth kingdom principle** we want to follow and consider is a **willingness to succeed**. *(2Corinthians 8:12)* says, "If there first be a willing mind, it is accepted according to what one has, and not according to what one does not have." To succeed in life one must have the right attitude. "As a man thinks so is he." God is not concerned about what one does not have. God will take what one has if we are first willing to offer what we have to Him. The lad did not have but two fish and five barley loaves of bread. He was willing to offer what he had to God. If we want to succeed as Christians we should not devalue what we have but be willing to offer what we have to God. God can take that which appears to man to be insufficient and make it sufficient if we are willing to offer it to Him. Moses had only a rod but he stretched forth his rod and God parted the Red Sea. David had only a sling shot but he offered it to God and defeated Goliath. George Washington Carver only knew how to grow peanuts and potatoes in Tuskegee, Alabama, but he had a philosophy, "Use what you have." He was determined to succeed and he took the peanuts and potatoes and developed over three hundred products.

The **sixth kingdom principle** we want to consider is **laying aside habits or anything that would come between you and God**. *(Hebrews 12:1)* says, "Let us lay aside every weight and sin that does so easily beset us, and let us run the race with patience, the race set before us." Jesus said, "If any man would come after Me, let him deny himself and take up the cross and follow Me." We have to bury some things that come between God and us. Jesus said if we are not willing to deny ourselves then we are not worthy of Him. Jesus said in *(Luke 18:28-29),* "No one who has left house, or parents or brother, sister or wife or children for the kingdom of God's sake, shall not receive manifold in this present time and in the world to come life everlasting." As Christians we cannot put old wine into new wineskins or put an old patch on a new garment. There are some things we must leave in our past. The Apostle Paul stated, "That this one thing I do forgetting those things that are behind me, and reaching forth for those things that are before me." We can learn from our past experiences whether they are good or bad. But the things that God has for each of us are ahead of us, not behind us. We honor the past but we cannot live in the past. We have to free ourselves of bad habits, bad relationships and anything that would hinder our spiritual growth.

The **seventh and final kingdom principle** we need to follow is to **plant a seed and water it**. As Christians we are to sow seeds. *(2 Corinthians 9:6)* says, "He which soweth sparingly shall also reap sparingly; and he which soweth bountifully shall reap also bountifully." We must sow into the lives of others. The church should sow into ministries outside of itself. We are to sow into fertile ground where the seed we sow will take root and will be nourished. (Ecclesiastes 11:1) says, "Cast thy bread upon the waters: for thou shalt find it after many days. When we sow we sow in obedience and faith." When we sow into the lives of others and other ministries we co-labor with others to build the kingdom of God. We are laborers together with God. One man plants, another waters but God will give the increase. When we sow we sow with faith and expectancy. When we sow we sow with expectancy, waiting for God to bring the harvest to past. We sow acknowledging God as our source. Well my brother, well my sister, let us not grow weary in well doing, for in due season we shall reap the harvest if we faint not, for in due season the sun will shine again.

In due season the weak will get stronger and the strong will become mightier. In due season night will return to day.

In due season midnight turns to daybreak. In due season, winter turns to springtime and springtime turns to summer.

In due season God restores what the enemy has taken from us, if we faint not.

In due season the storm passes over, if we faint not.

Therefore my beloved be steadfast, unmovable, always abounding in the work of the Lord, forasmuch, as ye know your labor is not in vain in the Lord.

13

Strengthen our Spiritual Immune System

(Ephesians 6:10-20)

We have been preaching and teaching on the Holy Spirit. We have learned that man is a trinity being: body, soul, and spirit. The body represents the embodiment of man, soul being the consciousness, mental and emotional state of man, and spirit representing the life of man. The Christian has both a physical and spiritual immune system. The function of the immune system is to defend the body against invaders. There are microbes (germs and other microorganisms) that can invade the body. Cancer cells and transplanted tissues and organs are all viewed by the immune system as intruders. These germs that enter our body must be attacked and defeated before they infiltrate the whole body. The immune system is based in the body's lymphatic system, and coordinates key body parts such as lymph nodes, tonsils, bone marrow, spleen, liver, lungs, and intestines to organize and deploy the antibody-producing cells to attack invaders. When an infection enters your body the lymphatic system kicks in and destroys the germs that cause infections. God has an immune system designed to protect and destroy external invaders that seek to weaken our spiritual immune system. There are people who take precautionary measures to protect the body from colds, flu and other viruses that attack our bodies. How we dress and what we wear when the weather changes will protect us from colds or the flu and possibly any other sickness. Doctors will tell you that exercise is good for the body, especially the heart. So many people and some being Christians are poor stewards of their bodies. They fail to watch what they eat. I believe that cancer comes from something we eat. Doctors also agree that cancer comes from something we eat. It starts with a virus that enters our body. There are certain vegetables we can eat that have certain antitoxins in them that fight cancer.

There are many people who fail to be good stewards of their spiritual immune system. There are external germs that will invade our spiritual lives, and if not checked, can create havoc in our lives. As Christians we have to defend ourselves against worldly germs everyday, if not they will take over our lives completely. There are financial shortfalls, breakdowns and breakups in relationships, vocational disruptions, family problems, natural disasters, accidents, discouragements, despair, loneliness, and even illnesses that seek to invade our spiritual immune system. When external germs or outside forces seek to invade our lives spiritually, each Christian needs to keep their spiritual immune system strengthened and built up to fight off viruses that lead to infections. Infections that affect our lives mentally, emotionally and spiritually and could bring about spiritual and physical death. When we neglect to exercise good discipline physically and spiritually we endanger our lives and expose ourselves to life-threatening consequences. We want to look at eight basic principles that will strengthen our spiritual immune system.

The **first principle we need to strengthen our spiritual immune system is spiritual devotion and study**. Reading and studying God's word will strengthen your spiritual immune system. *(2 Timothy 2:15)* says, "Study to show thyself approved unto God a workman needing to be a shame but rightly dividing the word of truth." The word of God is pure and it is a shield unto them that trust in Him. God's word shields us from the fiery darts of the wicked that will attempt to invade our lives. (Psalm 84:11) says, "For the Lord God is a sun and a shield; the Lord will give grace and glory; no good thing will He withhold from them that walk uprightly." When we develop a life of devotion God's word will give us light; that's what the word means when it says He is our sun. The sun gives us light, as the word is a lamp unto thy feet and a light unto thy pathway. When we have a devotional life the Lord will give us grace, meaning God will favor our lives with good. When we have devotion in our lives God will give us glory, meaning He will honor our lives with good things, and no good thing will He withhold from them that seek to walk uprightly according to His word.

The **second spiritual principle** we must have to strengthen our spiritual immune system is a strong prayer life. *(Luke 18:1)* says, "Man ought to always pray and faint not." If we would spend more time praying we would grow spiritually. If we would pray more on a daily basis we would be less inclined to faint when the forces of the enemy seek to invade our lives. We are to pray without ceasing, praying always with prayer and supplications. We are not just to pray, we are to be constant and fervent in prayer. *(James 5:16), says,* "The effectual fervent prayer of the righteous avails much*."* Prayer is one of our spiritual weapons which will enable us to cast down imagination and impure thoughts that seek to invade our minds and spirit. When we pray we pray according to the will of God and the word of God. *(Philippians 4:6-7)* says, "Be anxious for nothing but all things through prayer and supplication, with thanksgiving, let your request be made known unto God, and the peace of God which passes all understanding shall keep your heart and mind through Christ Jesus." We must pray for strength, pray for wisdom, pray for endurance, pray for guidance, pray for help, and pray for faithfulness to God's word and the work of God.

The **third spiritual principle that will strengthen our spiritual immune system is meditation**. God said to Joshua, "This book of the Law shall not depart out of your mouth, but thou shalt meditate upon it day and night, that thou may observe to do all that is written therein, and then thou shalt make that way prosperous and then thou shalt have good success." Meditation means to reflect on God's word. David said in *(Psalm 1:2),* "I will meditate day and night." "Thou will keep him in perfect peace whose mind is stayed on thee" *(Isaiah 26:3)*. David said in *(Psalm 27:13), "I would have fainted unless I believed that I would see the goodness of the Lord in the land of the living."* If we are to strengthen our spiritual immune system we must learn to meditate on the word of God. God's word tells us that when we are being tempted and tried, there is no temptation taken as such that is common to man, but God will always make a way of escape. We must encourage ourselves in the Lord as we meditate on His word.

The **fourth spiritual principle needed to strengthen our spiritual immune system is confession**. A clear conscience is conducive to one having a spiritually healthy life. If you are living with unresolved guilt your spiritual health is in danger. Guilt leads to physical complications and to spiritual ill health. If your life is cluttered with sin you need to come clean with God. Confession is acknowledging the wrong you have done to others and God. We must learn to confess our faults one to another as well as to God. *(Proverbs 28:13) says, "He who covers his sins shall not prosper; but whoso confesses and forsakes them shall have mercy." (1John 1:9) says, "If we confess our sins, He is faithful and just to forgive us our sins, and cleanse from all unrighteousness."* God has not dealt with us according to our sins neither has He rewarded us according to our iniquities, but as far as the east is from the west has He separated our sins from us. When we confess, acknowledge that we have done wrong, God will abundantly have mercy upon us. God is longsuffering toward us, not willing that any should perish but all come to repentance. If we have sinned we must do as David, confess, acknowledge to God that we have sinned and fallen short of His glory. We all have missed the mark.

The **fifth spiritual principle to strengthen your spiritual immune system is worship and church attendance**. To be healthy spiritually requires worshipping God on a regular basis. We were created to worship God and worshipping God is essential to strengthening our spiritual immune system. When we fail to worship God, it leads to isolation, alienation, and infection; the disease of self-centeredness sets in.

Worshipping God requires church attendance. *(Hebrews 10:25)* says, "Not forsaking the assembling of ourselves together, as is the manner of some, but exhorting one another, and so much the more as you see the day approaching." Church attendance is vital to spiritual growth. It strengthens the spiritual immune system. Worshipping God should not be based on one's feelings. Our church attendance should not be based on having a position of leadership in the church. If you only attend church because you are the leader of some board you are attending church for the wrong reason. Worship and church attendance is not about a position in the church; it's about God. We attend church to worship God who is worthy of all honor, praise and glory. Every Christian should be planted or located in some local church. The body is one, and has many members, and all the members of that one body being many, are one body: so also is Christ. God has set every member in the body as it pleased Him. Every one who becomes a member of the body of Christ becomes a part of the body and should help supply the body. When the members of the body come together we encourage one another in the faith. When the body of Christ comes together it becomes one body. Jesus prayed, in the priestly prayer in St. John 17,,that the disciples would be one as He and the Father were one. When we come together to worship God we declare our oneness.

The **sixth spiritual principle that will help strengthen our spiritual immune system is Service**. We are saved and called to serve. God has given every one a spiritual gift to serve. *(1 Peter 4:10)* says, "As each one has received a gift, minister it to one another, as good stewards of the manifold grace of God." If you are not using the gift God has given you to serve Him and others your spiritual immune system is clogged up. Jesus said, "If you love Me serve Me." We serve God and man when we make ourselves available to be used by God. The Greek word for service is "Diakonia" meaning service. We must understanding that if we are to serve God and do kingdom works we must have the right attitude. The psalmist says, "Serve the Lord with gladness." We must see the work or the service that we give as a labor of love. We are to serve God and one another. Whatever we do for God we are to do it heartily unto God, not unto men; knowing that of the Lord we shall receive the reward of the inheritance: for we serve the Lord Christ. (Colossians 3:23-24) The late Dr. Martin Luther King, Jr. said, "Everybody can be great because anybody can serve.

You don't have to have a college degree to serve. You don't have to make your subject and your verb agree to serve. You don't have to know Plato and Aristotle to serve. You don't have to know Einstein's Theory of Relativity to serve. You don't have to know the second theory of thermo-dynamics in physics to serve. You only need a heart full of grace. A soul generated by love."

The **seventh spiritual principle to strengthen our spiritual immune system is Giving**. Winston Churchill once said, "We make a living by what we get but we make a life by what we give." Giving starts with sowing. Investing, giving of your resources, time, talent, and treasure is a healthy investment into your spiritual immune system. Giving deals with being a good steward with what God has given you. Most people and some being Christians are poor managers of what God has entrusted to them. Giving is a part of worship. When you come to worship God and you fail to give God His tithe your worship is not complete. We reap what we sow physically and spiritually. Some people are not only physically bankrupt but they are spiritually bankrupt. (Luke 6:38) says, "Give and it shall be given unto you, good measure, pressed down, shaken together, and running over, men will pour into your blossom." (2Corinthians 9:7) says, "Every man according as he purposes in his heart, so let him give, not grudgingly, nor of necessity: for God loves a cheerful giver. And God is able to make all grace abound toward you always having all sufficiency in all things, may abound to every good work." When we give to God, God will see that all our needs are met and that we will not lack for anything that's according to his will and purpose.

The **eighth and final principle that will strengthen our spiritual immune system is fellowship with other Christians**. The Greek word for fellowship is "Koinonia", it means having things in common. Fellowship was one of the defining features and characteristics of the New Testament church. *(Acts 2:44)* says, "Now all who believed were together and had all things in common." As Christians, we are members of the body of Christ. We are connected one with another in the body. When we are disconnected from the body our spiritual immune system is vulnerable. The church has to work together, pray together, worship together, study together, serve together and love one another. We are one in the Spirit; we are one in the Lord. We will walk hand in hand, we will walk hand in hand and they will know that we are Christians by our love, by our love and they will know that we are Christians by our love.

14

The Church God Is Building

(Psalm 127:1, Matthew 16:13-20)

When we talk about the church, we discover and learn that there are many different views about what the church is or is not. However, apart from the word of God, meaning the bible, our understanding as to what the church is, is limited. Throughout the bible the life of the believer is compared to the construction of a building or an edifice. Jesus said that He would build His church, and the gates of hell shall not prevail against it. The church being the body of Christ is a building under construction. The philosophical term "existentialism" means we are in a constant state of becoming. It does not yet appear what we shall be, but we know that when He shall appear, we shall be like Him. If we as Christians are growing we are always in a state of becoming. The bible talks about the church as a building that's under construction.

In the Epistle of Jude verse twenty says, "Building up yourselves on your most holy faith." In (*First Corinthians 3:9-10*), Paul says, "Ye are God's building." In (*Ephesians 2:7*), Paul says, "Rooted and built up in Christ, and established in the faith." In (*Acts 20:32),* it says, in regard to the Elders of the church, "The word of God's grace is able to build you up." All of these passages of scripture make reference to the believer's life as a building under construction or being constructed. In the natural as well as the spiritual order of life, the first and most important element of the building is the foundation. The foundation sets the limits to the weight and height of the building. There is a fixed relationship between the foundation and the building. The church is to be about kingdom building; bringing the kingdom of God to earth as it is in heaven. The church is to be about making disciples of all people. One of the major concerns that I have about the church is its lack of understanding about its calling. The church has a calling to fulfill. The church is not a body or institution in and of itself. It is not my church or your church per se; it is God's church. Every church is to serve its present age and to fulfill it's calling during its age. As the body of Christ, the church as an institution is to empower it members by teaching what the mission of the church is all about; if it is to serve the present age.

The church ultimately belongs to God, its founder. Jesus said, "That He would build His church." He did not say that He would build His people a church, but He would build His church. The church cannot be invaded by the world. It is in the world but not of the world. The church is to invade the world instead of the world invading the church. The church is to be about transforming the world instead of the world transforming the church. It is time we ask ourselves as church leaders, "Is America in the church or is the church in America?" The only conforming the church should be doing is conforming to the will and word of God. The Apostle Paul in *(Philippians 3:10)* says, ". . . Being made conformable unto His death."

All too often the church conforms to the world. When we conform to the death of Christ, then our lives will be transformed into the likeness of Jesus the Christ. The word conform is a process of metamorphosis as that of the butterfly. As we conform to the death of Jesus Christ transformation takes place in our lives. We become like Him.

We are changed; we become a new creation, created for good works. Jesus would build His church to continue His ministry here on earth. Jesus made a declaration upon the confession of Peter that He was the Christ, the Son of the living God. Thou art Peter, (Petros) and upon the (Petra), I will build My Church and the gates of hell would not prevail against it. There is a similarity in sound between these two words. Their meanings are quite different. Petros means a small stone or pebble. Petra means a large rock.

The idea of Jesus building His church upon a pebble or stone was not what Jesus was talking about. Peter was petros - a little stone or pebble. Jesus is not identifying Peter with the rock: on the contrary, He is contrasting Peter with the rock. He is showing the difference between a rock and a stone. Jesus is telling Peter that the petros, a little stone, is insufficient to build His church on. He would build His church on the Petra, the stone. Jesus knew that He could not build His church on the Apostle Peter. Peter, before he was converted, was like many people in the church today. He was not stable-minded or steadfast. He would straddle the fence. He would follow Jesus only so far and then would follow Him afar off. He would say one thing but do something else. He would deny Jesus three times. If one has not been truly converted one will deny Christ as Peter did. One will deny Him their time, their talents, their gifts, their loyalty and their love. Peter would allow himself to be influenced by others. How could Jesus build His church on a person with such a fickle and flawed character? We have many Peters in the church, which have not been converted. When a person has truly been converted they are convicted when they realize they are wrong. They can be corrected without getting an attitude. What would Jesus build His church on? What is the church? Some people believe the church is brick and mortar. The church Jesus would build would not be of a material substance. We have direction as to how Jesus would build His church. We have a blueprint in the book of Acts.

The **first pillar** God uses to build His church is the foundation. The apostle Paul stated, "For no other foundation can no man lay than that which is laid, Jesus Christ." Jesus is the foundation the church is built on. The church lives not because people live but because Christ lives. Christ is the head of the church. The apostle Paul cautioned the hearer that we must be careful how we build upon the foundation that has been laid. The apostle Paul would have us know that anything we attempt to build upon the foundation will be tried by fire and the fire will reveal what types of works are being laid upon the foundation. Many churches feel that to grow the church, we must use worldly tactics. The church is to be in the world but not of the world. The church's one foundation is Jesus Christ our Lord; He is the new creation by water and the blood.

The **second pillar** that was essential to the birth of the church was the **Holy Spirit**. In the book of Acts we see the promise of the Holy Spirit being fulfilled. A church without the Holy Spirit cannot survive or thrive. *(John 6:63)* says, "It is the spirit that gives life: the flesh profits nothing; the words that I speak unto you, they spirit and they are life." If the church is to be the church God intended it to be it needs the power of the Holy Spirit. The church's only power source is the Holy Spirit. The church God is building is led by the spirit, filled with the spirit, guided by the spirit, taught by the spirit, convicted by the spirit, and led into all truth by the Holy Spirit. The church has to have the empowerment of the Holy Spirit. The Holy Spirit is what gave birth to the church on the day of Pentecost. The Holy Spirit is both personal and non personal. It works within the believer and outside of the believer. The Holy Spirit is the church's power source. I once asked a man who was a deacon in his church what was the church's source of power and his reply was the deacon board. The church's power is not limited to a board or any individual. The wind blows where it wills and we hear and see the sound but cannot tell from whence it comes so is it with the Holy Spirit. The Holy Spirit is the church's power source.

The **third pillar** God uses to build His church is the teaching and preaching of God's word. When Peter preached, *(Acts 2:41)* says, "They gladly received his word, were baptized and the same day there were added unto them three thousand souls." The Word of God builds the church as well as builds up the church. The scripture says, "He that hears my word and believes on him that has sent me shall have eternal life." The word of God must be preached to the end that someone is saved. A church that does not preach the word will not stand. Paul said, "If any man preaches anything other than Christ let him be a curse." Paul said, "It pleased God by the foolishness of preaching to save them that believe." Paul said to Timothy, Preach the word, be instant in season and out of season, rebuke, reprove, correct and exhort. When the word of God is preached it must be preached in such a way the simple can understand the message of salvation. "The entrance of thy words gives light; it gives understanding unto the simple" (Psalm 119:130). The word must be taught where it speaks to the human condition that is relevant to the times. The word speaks of God becoming flesh and dwelling among us.

The fourth **pillar** that builds God's church is **persevering in the Word**. *(Acts 2:42)* says, "And they continued steadfastly in the Apostles doctrine." The church has to remain faithful to the word of God. A church in Concord, NC started a ministry some years ago, but since its beginning it has died. The people left the word of God and went about doing things not according to the word. A church without the word of God cannot withstand the gates of hell. I read a book some years ago where a church in Houston, Texas was started and a building was later built. The members of the church came together and laid the carpet on the concrete floor. As they were cleaning the concrete floor and getting it ready to lay the carpet, one of the members suggested to the pastor that each member write their favorite scripture on the floor before the carpet was laid. The moral to the story or message is that if the church God is building is going to stand it must be built on the word of God if it is to withstand the gates of hell. The word says, heaven and earth will pass away but My word will abide forever. The word is a lamp unto my feet and a light unto my path. The word is sharper than any two edged sword. The grass withers the flowers fade but the word of our God shall stand forever. The church is built on the Word of God.

The **fifth pillar** that God uses to build His church is **faithfulness**. *Revelation 2: 10)* speaks of the church at Smyrna where they met opposition from outside forces and they were persecuted for what they believed. The church God is building is called to be faithful unto death. The church God is building is to be faithful in all things, not just some things but in all things. Jesus, in the parable of the talents, talked about the servants being faithful over a few things and He would make them rulers over many things. Faith and faithfulness go together. The church God is building is faithful to its calling. The church God is building is faithful to its mission; to go into all the world and preach and teach all people baptizing them in the name of the Father and the Son and the Holy Spirit. The church God is building believes in walking worthy of its calling. The church God is building is faithful in meeting the needs of the least of these. The church God is building is faithful to the great commission to go beyond its borders and go into the hedges and by ways and compel men and women to come to the Savior. Jesus told the church at Smyrna to be "Thou faithful unto death and He would give them a crown of life." A church that is faithful to God abounds with blessings. God will say to the church that has been faithful unto death, "Well done thou good and faithful servant; because thou hast been faithful over a few things I will make thee ruler over many things."

The **sixth pillar** God is using to build His church is that it will have one fold and one Shepard. In

(*St. John 10:* 16) Jesus said, "And other sheep I have that are not of this fold: them also I must bring, and they shall hear My voice; and there shall be one fold and one Shepard." This verse would have us to know that the church God is building is not limited to any one denomination or religious group. There will be Methodist, Baptist, Presbyterians, Church of God, and the Church of God in Christ, Church of God of Prophecy, Roman Catholic, Episcopalians, all denominations and non-denominations - all churches that confess Jesus Christ as Lord and savior. There will be one fold and one Shepard of all the sheep regardless of their denominational point of reference. The book of Revelation, the twenty-first chapter verses 12-15, speaks of twelve gates to the city. The interpretation of this verse is that God has more than one way, meaning no one single denomination is the only way for one to get to God. God can use whatever denomination He pleases to bring the message of salvation to the world. God is not limited to any denomination. When the church is married to the lamb there will be the consummation of the church. No more barriers to divide us, for we shall be like Him. When we all get to heaven what a day of rejoicing it will be, when we all see Jesus we'll sing and shout the victory.

The **seventh and final pillar** God uses to build His church upon is **Unity**. Jesus stated in His priestly prayer in *(St. John 17:1), "That they may be one meaning the disciples would be one, as He and the Father were one."* Jesus prayed that there would be unity among the disciples and the church. *(Acts 2:46)* says, "And they, continuing daily with one accord in the temple, and breaking of bread from house to house, did eat their meat with gladness and singleness of heart." When there was unity on the day of Pentecost the Holy Spirit came like a mighty rushing wind. The Apostle Paul stated that we should endeavor to keep the unity of the spirit in the bond of peace. There is unity in the Godhead. There is one body, one Spirit, one hope, one Lord, one, faith, one baptism, one God and Father of us all, and through all and in all. Till we come in the unity of the faith, and the knowledge of the Son of God, unto a perfect man, unto the measure of the stature of the fullness of Christ, till we grow up in all things, which is the head, even Christ. When unity comes every stain will be washed away. Until we come to the unity of the faith, every storm has passed over; till we come to the unity of the faith, every tear has been wiped away. And we shall know as we are known. Thanks be to God who always causes us to triumph in Christ Jesus.

15

The Power and Passion of Pentecost

(Acts 2:1-13)

The day of Pentecost was an annual Jewish festival or time of harvest. The word Pentecost means fifty; fifty days after the Passover feast people from all nations would come together and bring the first fruits of their harvest to Jerusalem. God in His providential will fulfilled the promise of the Holy Spirit on the day of Pentecost. Jesus told His Disciples that He would send them another comforter who would abide with them forever. When He, the Holy Spirit would come, He would teach them, He would lead them, He would guide them into all truth, and He would convict them and bring all things to their remembrance. So on the day of Pentecost we see the words of Jesus being fulfilled. The most significant thing about Pentecost was when the Holy Spirit descended. Power and Passion were given to the apostles on the day of Pentecost. The apostles would first serve their apprenticeship as disciples when they were with Jesus but now they would go forth as apostles to continue the work that Jesus had begun. The mission of the church is to continue the work Jesus begun. An apostle is one who is sent forth. The apostles could not go forth without the proper power and authority. They would now go forth with power and authority to establish the church that Jesus said He would build.

The church is not a physical building it is a container. The reason most buildings we call churches are not being used is because the buildings are just containers. A container is an instrument we use when we have a need or use for it. Some people don't have much need for the church (they called the building) because they are very seldom seen at, or involved in, the church. The church is the body of Christ and the building is where the body of Christ meets. The church's mission is to make disciples of all people. If the church is not making Disciples the church is not fulfilling its mission or purpose. When a church fails to grow there is something wrong with its power and passion. Jesus told His Disciples they would receive power after the Holy Spirit comes upon them; they would be His witnesses. The word "witness" comes from the Greek word Matura, which means martyr. A martyr or a witness is one who has experienced or witnessed an event. The Holy Spirit is a person, not in the sense that He is flesh and bones, but in personality. When God was revealed in the flesh He was revealed as Son of Man and Son of God. The Holy Spirit now is the personality of God the Father and God the Son. Many people are quick to say that the Holy Spirit is a feeling. We cannot limit the presence of God to a feeling. Just because you do not feel happy or jubilant does not mean that the Holy Spirit is not present. Why is it that the church has lost the power and passion it had on the day of Pentecost? Jesus said to His disciples that greater works they would do. Many churches today are like the church of the Laodiceans in the book of Revelation. Christ was on the outside knocking and wanting to come in, but the people on the inside felt they had everything and did not need Christ. The church at Laodicea, was neither hot nor cold, it was lukewarm. Many churches today feel they have everything based on their individual status. Christ is nonexistent or a non-player. Many churches have a form of Godliness but there is no power or passion that will impact the world. It does not have the power that brings about signs and wonders. It has lost its savor. There is more of the world in the church and less of the church in the world. Jesus said, "Be in the world but not of the world." The church is to bring about transformation to the world. The church is not to conform to the world but to transform the world. "And be not conformed to the world but be ye transformed by the renewing of your mind that ye may prove what is good and acceptable and the perfect will of God." (Romans, 12:2) I recently talked with a person who had joined a church and he stated he joined the church to come out of the world. But to his surprise he discovered that a lot of the world was in the church and he was confused.

The story is told about a church that had caught fire and burned down and a club owner in the community offered the church it's building until the church was rebuilt. One night, a man in the club fell asleep and woke up the next morning lying under a table. The man, who was intoxicated, woke up due to the singing and preaching. When the invitation was extended the man came down the isle to join the church and the pastor asked the man if he had anything he wanted to say. He stated to the pastor that he did have something he wanted to say; that some of the people in the choir were some of the same ones who were in the club the night before. The man went on to say the only difference was that they were wearing different clothing and singing different songs. The church received the power and passion at Pentecost. The church, embodied in the Apostles, went forth with power and passion. When a church or a Christian has power and passion it bears fruit. It brings results and souls are saved. Peter preached and three thousand souls were added to the church in the aftermath of Pentecost. There are **five premises** I want to suggest as to why the church lacks power and passion.

The **first premise** we want to examine is a lack of faith and confidence in the resurrected Christ. Many people in the church lack faith and confidence in God. Many people lack faith and the assurance they need to do the work of God. Many people are not convinced that Jesus said, "Without Me you can do nothing." Many people have more confidence in their job than they do God. Many people believe their job is their source instead of acknowledging God as their source. Some people have more confidence in their education than in God. Parents tell their children they need to get an education, and that's fine, but education can only carry you but so far. Education and a job have their place but they do not bring total happiness. Many people want the things of God but they want them on their terms. Many people use His name only in a crisis, as if God comes only when they call Him. If they don't need Him they won't call Him or serve Him. But the Apostle Paul stated, "I am persuaded that He is able to keep that which I have committed unto Him unto that day." Jesus Christ is the all-sufficient one.

The **second premise** we want to examine concerning the lack of power and passion in the church is a *lack of conviction*. Jesus said when the Holy Spirit comes He will convict us of all sin. Every Apostle Jesus called and used was convicted of his sin. The role of the Holy Spirit is to lead us into all truth. If one is living in sin and not convicted of his sin and not willing to do something about his sin or fails to repent, then one becomes an enemy of the cross.

Sin robs us of our power and passion. You may sing but there is no power or passion in your singing. You may pray but there is no power or passion in the prayer. The scriptures teach us that we cannot serve two masters; we will love one and hate the other. King David realized that when he was convicted of his sin; God's spirit was no longer present with him. He realized that he had lost the joy of his salvation, and he asked God to take not his Holy Spirit from him, but to create in him a clean heart. The Holy Spirit will bring about the conviction of sin. Ye shall know the truth and the truth shall make you free. The truth will bring about the conviction of moral and spiritual sins.

The **third premise** we want to examine with regard to the lack of power and passion in the church is a need for a true conversion. A true conversion brings about a genuine change in a person's life. Jesus called Peter to follow Him; but until he was really converted there was no real change in his life. Before Peter was converted he denied Jesus; he would say one thing but do something else. He had a violent temper; he was hot headed and would curse. Jesus told Peter, "When you are converted strengthen your brother." But when he was truly converted the world saw a new man. He preached at Pentecost and three thousand souls were added to the church. When a person has been truly converted there will be results. If your life and faith is not impacting the lives of others something is wrong with your conversion. Repentance is a change of one's ways but conversion is a change of the heart, which will be reflected in one's ways, or conduct. In *(Acts 4: 13)* we read; "Now when they saw the boldness of Peter and John, and perceived that they were unlearned and ignorant men, they marveled, and they took knowledge that they had been with Jesus." When one has been with Jesus or had an experience with Jesus others will see the change.

The **fourth premise** that speaks to the lack of power and passion in the church is a *lack of* commitment to living what we say we believe and know to be the truth. Commitment means 'unto' not 'until'. We have a lot of 'until' so called Christians in the church. Many people make commitments and fail to live up to the commitments they make. Many people make too many excuses for not being committed to God and His church. Many people are committed until they are challenged to live up to their commitments. They get mad and quit when they are confronted. Many are committed until they can no longer have things their way. Commitment means to do, to work, to give without reservations, to give unconditionally, and to go beyond the point of no return. Commitment starts with God. Commitment means doing something when it is not only convenient for you to do it. When one is a committed Christian, it means they are committed to the things of God, His word, His work, His cause and His church. Paul said to Timothy in *(2 Timothy 1:12),* "For I know in whom I have believed, and am persuaded that he is able to keep that which I have committed unto him against that day. Being a Christians is the ultimate commitment." Jesus said, "Be thou faithful unto death."

The fifth and final premise we want to examine as to why there is a lack of power and passion in the church is the lack of consecration. If the church is not consecrated to its mission, purpose, and calling there will be no power and passion. Power comes when we consecrate ourselves to God. If we want power we need to be consecrated to prayer, to study, and to preparation. We must be consecrated to a life of holiness. Without holiness no man can see the Lord. Consecration brings dedication and dedication brings consecration. Many people in the church do not have a passion for God. The story is told of a gazelle, one of the fastest animals in the lion family. It has been said that the speed of a gazelle can top out at eighty to eighty-five miles per hour. When the gazelle spots its prey it launches its attack. If the gazelle does not catch him when he reaches his top speed he will not prevail. Why? The gazelle's heart is not that large and he loses momentum. Well, that is the way it is with some Christians; their heart is not big enough and consecrated to God. They do not have the passion for the things of God.

Consecrate me now to thy service Lord by the power of grace divine, let my soul look up with a steadfast hope and my will be lost in thine. Draw me nearer, nearer, nearer blessed Lord to the cross where thou hast died, draw me nearer, nearer Lord to thy precious bleeding side.

16

The Seven W's of the
Christian Faith

(James 2:14-26)

The number s*even* in the bible deals with perfection or completeness. The number seven begins in the book of Genesis. There were *seven* days involved in the creation. In Leviticus the twenty-third chapter we see that there were *seven* major feasts in Israel's life. In the Lord's Prayer there are *seven* petitions. In the thirteenth chapter of Matthew there are *seven* parables, which detail the completeness of the kingdom. There are the *seven* last words or sayings of the cross. In Ephesians four, we see the *seven* one's of the Church. "One body, One hope, One Spirit, One Lord, One faith, One baptism, One God and Father of us all, who is above all and through all and in all.." In the book of revelations we see *seven* churches. Seven stars, Seven Angels, Seven golden candlesticks, seven seals, and seven bowls of God's wrath. The book of revelation speaks of seven trumpets, seven visions and seven angels with seven plagues. Seven deals with completion or perfection. God calls us not only to salvation He calls us to live our faith by embracing certain disciplines or principles, which make our faith credible. We are called to live our faith by embodying the fruits of the spirit. Faith and Salvation work hand in hand. Salvation comes by grace through faith. There is a difference between saving faith and working faith. Some people have saving faith but they do not have a working faith. We must live our faith to let the world know that we are saved. I want to talk about the seven W's of the Christian faith. Our faith should be seen or demonstrated through these seven W's.

The **first 'W'** we want to examine which supports our faith is **Work**. *(James 2:14)* tells us "That faith without work is dead." As Christians we are instructed to work. However our works do not save us, but is evidence of our faith. We are saved by grace alone through faith. Our faith ought to produce works of repentance. Our works are fruits of our faith in action. Our works are the wheels to make our faith authentic. Our works are the wheels that mobilize our faith. Faith alone is not enough if it does not bear fruit. "Works" partners with our faith. Every Christian must have a mind to work for God. We do not work for our salvation, but we work because of our salvation. "By grace ye have been saved, that not of yourself, it's the gift of God, not of works lest any man should boast." *(Ephesians 2: 8-9)* *(Ephesians 2:10)* tells us, "For we are His workmanship, created in Christ Jesus for good works, which God prepared beforehand that we should walk in them." Jesus told His Disciples that greater works they would do. We are to be co-laborers with God and with one another.

The **second 'W'** of the Christian faith is **Walk**. For we walk by faith and not by sight. When we talk about the Christian's walk we are talking about his conduct and lifestyle. We are admonished by the word of God as to how we ought to walk. In *(Genesis 17:1),* God said to Abraham, "I am the almighty God; walk before Me and be blameless." The Christian's walk of faith is outlined in the Word of God. Walk in love, show love one to another and show the world God's love. Walk worthy of your calling with which you were called. To walk worthy means, whatever God has called us to do we need to present ourselves suitable and fitting for that calling. If we are called to fatherhood or motherhood we need to walk worthy of the calling. We are to uphold the dignity and honor of whatever our calling is in life. Walk circumspectly; circumspectly means we must be careful how we talk, where we go, and how we conduct ourselves as Christians. Walk as children of light. Wherever we go we should let our light so shine that men will see our good works and God will be glorified in heaven. Whenever we walk we are to bring light to someone who has lost his or her way.

The **third 'W'** of the Christian faith is **Worship**. Worship is important to God. We are to worship only God; "Thou shalt have no other God before Me." Worship means to ascribe worth and value to God because He is worthy. In *(John 4:23-24)* we read, "But the hour is coming, and is, when the true worshippers will worship the Father in spirit and in truth; for the Father seeks such to worship Him." Making a lot of noise is not worshipping Him in spirit and in truth. We worship not only with our lips but worship involves the heart. When we worship God we bless Him. "Bless the Lord O my soul and all that is within me, bless His holy name." Worship is to be an experience where we come together to worship God. We praise Him for what He has done in our lives, but we worship Him for who He is. We worship God in our giving of thanks. We worship God when we place nothing above Him. We worship God when we give back to Him. We worship God when we bring the sacrifice of praise into His house. We worship God when we come into His presence as Isaiah did and was quicken to his holiness. We worship God when we present ourselves before Him as a living sacrifice.

The **fourth 'W'** of the Christian faith is **Witnessing**; Jesus told His Apostles in *(Acts 1:8),* "That they would be witnesses of Him in Jerusalem, Judea, Samaria, and uttermost part of the world." We witness as much by how we live as well as what we say. Our works bear witness of who Jesus Christ is in our lives. Jesus told His Disciples, "To love one another, and by this men will know that they are His Disciples." We must tell a dying world that Jesus saves. Witnessing means we share with others what God has done in each of our lives. All too often we talk about what we have done and fail to recognize what God has done. Jesus said, "If I be lifted up from the earth I will draw all men unto me."

I remember some years ago talking with a man who had given his life to God. His life prior to coming to saving faith in Jesus Christ had been a life of drug addiction. He went on to tell me that one evening he was tempted to commit suicide because he felt that life was no longer worth living. He had become a slave to his addiction and he had hurt so many people who had tried to help him. He stated that he had stolen from them and he found himself homeless. He went on to say that as he attempted suicide, he put a gun to his head and pulled the trigger, the gun would not fire. He tried to pull the trigger three times but still, it would not fire. He asked God to save him and come into his life and deliver him from his drug addiction. He felt the presence of God come over his life and he was set free from drugs. Many of his friends saw the change in his life as he began to witness to them. He went on to tell me that many of his friends said to him that if God could change him they knew God could change them. One Sunday, at his church, twelve of his friends came to church and gave their lives to God. As Christians we are called to be witnesses. Our lives should bear witness to the saving power of Jesus Christ.

The **fifth 'W'** of the Christian faith is to Win souls for Christ. *(Proverb 11:30)* says, "He that wins souls is wise." We should live our lives in such a way that we win others for Christ to save. The Apostle Paul says in *(1 Corinthians 9:22),* "For I have become all things to all men, that I might by all means save some." To the Jew, I became a Jew that I might win Jews. "I have made myself a servant to all, that I might win the more." To the weak I became weak that I might win the weak. We never win souls for Christ by being racial bigots. The church cannot win souls for Christ by condemning people who are not like we are. To win souls for Christ we must meet people where they are. We meet people at their point of need. We do not have to change the message to win souls for Christ. Jesus is the same today, yesterday, and forever. We do not have to manipulate the word, all we have to do to win souls for Christ is to be real and show people the love of God. It is our responsibility to win our loved ones to Christ. I remember when I was pasturing in Birmingham, Alabama and would go downtown to get my hair cut every other Saturday morning. One morning I was walking down the streets of the city and I made the comment to my barber that many of the major churches in the city had died out. The young barber's reply was, reverend, people get tired of going to church hearing the preacher say you are going to hell and you need to be saved. He went on to say what I need is somebody to show me what being saved is and to stop telling me I'm going to hell. Show me what salvation is and maybe I will get saved. We win souls for Christ by showing people compassion and the love Christ offers them.

The **sixth 'W'** of the Christian faith is **Watch**. (1Corinthians 16:13) says, "Watch, stand fast in the faith, be brave, and be strong." (1 Peter 5:8) says, "Be sober, be vigilant, meaning be watchful; because your adversary the devil walks about as a roaring lion seeking whom he may devour." Watch as well as pray. We must watch our attitude, watch our walk, watch our talk, watch our language, and watch our conversation. We must watch our lifestyle, "Be in the world but not of the world." We must watch the company we keep. *(Proverb 13:20)* says, "He that walks with wise men shall be wise but a companion of fools shall be destroyed." It's the job of the pastor to watch over the flock of God. (Hebrews 13: 17) says, "Obey them that have rule over, and submit yourselves: for they watch over your souls, as they must give account that they do it with joy, and not with grief; for that is unprofitable for you." The church must watch the message it preaches and teach the whole counsel of God. God is not only a God of prosperity he is the God of the oppressed, and the God of the least of these.

The **seventh and final 'W'** of the Christian faith is to **Wait.** God calls us to wait on Him. There will be times in our lives when we have prayed, when we have worked hard, and it seems that things just don't get any better. We are told in *(Galatians 6:9)*, "And let us not grow weary in well doing: for in due season we shall reap if we faint not." I remember when I was a pastor in the A.M.E. Zion church over ten years ago. At an annual conference in Birmingham, Alabama there was a lady who gave her testimony. She had been coming to the annual conference for over thirteen years expecting to receive an appointment to a church but to her surprise and disappointment she never received an appointment. The previous year she had received an appointment to a church and she reported that she had come faithfully for thirteen years before she had ever received an appointment. She stated that the church she was appointed to had only three or four members but she was grateful for the three or four and they meant more to her than if she had had four or five hundred. Each year she came expecting a church and was disappointed but she continued to come and wait and she was finally given a church.

But Isaiah (40:28) says: "Hast thou not known? Hast thou not heard? The everlasting God, the Lord, The Creator of the ends of the earth, neither faints nor is weary. There is no searching of His understanding. He gives power to the weak, and to them that have no might, He increases strength. Even the youth shall faint, and be weary and the young men shall utterly fall, But they that wait upon the Lord, Shall renew their strength. They shall mount up with wings as eagles. They shall run and not be weary; they shall walk and not faint."

Wait I say on the Lord and be of good courage and He shall strengthen thine heart.

17

The Ultimate Commitment

(Luke 9:51-56)

On Palm Sunday God presented Himself in the person of Jesus Christ. Jesus' presentation of God as He journeyed to Jerusalem began before He made His final entry. His journey had many implications. Jesus would enter Jerusalem on three different occasions. He would first enter on the Sabbath. He entered the temple as a Priest and goes in and sees if the temple was in order and ousts moneychangers if necessary. His second entry into Jerusalem would be on Sunday, the first day of the week. On this occasion He would enter as King. He would enter the temple and cleanse the temple by ousting the moneychangers. His third journey to Jerusalem would be on Monday the second day of the week. On His third and final journey to Jerusalem He would enter as a Prophet and weep over the city. As a prophet He would prophesy of the future destruction of the temple and the city. His final journey was about commitment, the ultimate commitment.

Our text would have us know that Jesus was committed to the mission that was assigned to Him. "Now it came to pass, when the time had come for Him to be received up, that He steadfastly set His face to go to Jerusalem" *(Luke 9:51)*. Doing the work and will of God does not come without commitment. Jesus talked about commitment when it came to doing the will of God in emphatic terms. "I must work the works of Him that has sent me for night comes when no man can work." He said to His parents when He was a young boy when they had lost Him for a few days, "Did you not know that I must be about my father's business." Commitment involves completing what one starts. Finishing the work we have begun requires commitment. Jesus had the courage to face the city of Jerusalem. He did not run from or shun the commitment He had to fulfill. He knew there would be fierce obstacles He would have to face. Many did not receive Him the scripture tells us because His face was set for the journey to Jerusalem.

Commitment does not come without challenges. Facing the things we fear most measures our commitment. Commitment involves forgoing what we would sometimes do and surrendering to another's will. Jesus has demonstrated commitment to us when He was willing to become obedient to the father's will. *(Philippians 2:8)* deals with the kenosis doctrine where it says, "He became obedient unto death even the death of the cross." This passage demonstrates the ultimate commitment. He was willing to die to His will and fulfill the will of God the death of the cross. There are many things in life that, if it's to be successful, will take commitment. If a marriage is to be viable and successful it will require both parties being committed; committed to upholding the vows that were made. Raising children to be disciplined and respectful requires commitment on the part of both parents. If it takes two people to conceive a child then it takes two to raise the child. Many children have been raised in single parent homes and have been raised well. However children need both parents involved in their lives and this takes commitment. A college education requires commitment. It does not matter how gifted or talented an individual may be, if they are not committed to developing themselves their ability will carry them only so far. Some people are not committed to anything in life. And they wonder why they have not succeeded at anything in life. When one lacks commitment one can only go so far in life. One of the things we noticed about the crowd on Palm Sunday was that it was a fickle crowd. They called His name, but their loyalties were far from Him. They went through the motions of religion, but they lacked real loyalty and affection for Christ. Is this not the way it is with many of the people in the church? They sing anthems and praises to God on Sunday morning but they demonstrate no solemn commitment in their hearts. The people who made up the crowd were religious without being religious. They were performers but not true participants. They had a form of Godliness and lived by their wits instead of their faith. Many had no personal convictions or commitment they were caught up in the hype of the crowd. We discover that regardless of the fickleness of the crowd it did not impact Jesus and His commitment. The scripture tell us that He was rejected because of his commitment. *(Luke 9:53)* says, "They did not receive Him, because His face was set for the journey to Jerusalem." Jesus demonstrates to us that we should not allow what others do or fail to do to determine our commitment. Jesus teaches us that our ultimate commitment should be to God, not man.

The **first things** we must understand about commitment is that it involves work and one being willing to work diligently by applying oneself; not settling for anything than the best that God would have them to be and what God has called them to do. This involves work, effort continuously. Jesus said, "If ye continue in My word, Ye shall know the truth and the truth shall make you free." Commitment involves consistent application to completing and perfecting whatever God has entrusted to them. This means family, your relationship with your spouse and your children. Commitment involves time and energy. We can make some things happen, if we work hard enough, or God will make them happen.

The **second thing** that involves commitment is being steadfast. The problem with many people when it comes to being committed is that they are not steadfast. They are easily moved or sidetracked. They allow the least little thing to easily beset them. Commitment does not come without setbacks and disappointments. Commitment does not come without test and trials. Commitment requires us to be faithful unto, not until. *(1 Corinthians 15:58)* says, "Therefore, my beloved, be steadfast, immovable, always abounding in the work of the Lord." Jesus was steadfast in his commitment to go to Jerusalem and finish His work.

The **third thing** involved in commitment is sacrifice. Jesus demonstrated to us that the ultimate commitment required God to make a sacrifice. "For God so loved the world that He gave His only begotten Son, that whosoever believes in Him should not perish but have eternal life" (John 3:16). Sacrifice means that we must be willing to give up something that will cost us something. David said to the A-rau'nah in *(2 Samuel 24: 24),* "That he would not offer to God anything that did not cost him something." Jesus was committed to going as far as He needed to go to redeem humanity. He who knew no sin became sin, because He was committed. He who was rich became poor, because He was committed. He suffered the just for the unjust, because He was committed. "For when we were yet without hope, in due season Christ died for the ungodly because He was committed." He was committed to making a way for man to be reconciled back to God.

The **fourth thing** involved in commitment is remaining focused. The text says, "He set His face steadfastly to go to Jerusalem." He was focused on what was ahead of Him. What was ahead of Him was not a pretty picture. He would have to face betrayal by one of His own. He would be denied by one of His own but He was willing to stay focused and face many disappointments. He would face rejection and disbelief when He arrived in the city of Jerusalem. He would weep over the city due to their lack of faith. He remained focused on the cross that awaited Him. Being focused requires one to be committed to their assignment. Commitment starts with one having an inward conviction first. One heart is made up, one mind is made up and one is determined to hold out unto the end.

The **fifth and final thing** involved in the ultimate commitment is endurance. Commitment requires that one have endurance as well as perseverance. Both endurance and perseverance support or under gird one another. Many people do not have the will to endure or persevere through their hardships. (Hebrews 12:2) states that Jesus could see the joy that was set before Him which enabled Him to endure the cross, despising the shame. Endurance means to have the mental, physical and emotional stamina to persevere, meaning work through difficulty and pain. The ultimate commitment challenges us to keep going when we would want to quit. The one thing that God does not tolerate in us is quitting on the job or quitting our assignment. We have to know that weeping may endure for a night but joy comes in the morning. We must endure unto the end but there is a bright side somewhere. We must know that God is faithful and He has promised never to leave us nor forsake us. We have to endure hardness as a good soldier of Jesus Christ and run the race with patience unto Him the author and finisher of our faith.

The story is told about a master musician who went to his studio each day to practice for his annual recital. There was a young boy who sat outside his studio each day that he arrived. One day the young boy told the master musician that he wanted to learn how to play the piano. The master musician invited the young boy to his studio and he spent many days teaching him to play the piano until he felt that he was ready for his own musical recital. The master musician scheduled a recital for the young boy and invited his friends to come. As the young lad played and was applauded by the crowd he never turned around and bowed to the crowd. A friend of the master musician was surprised that the young lad would never turn and bow to the crowd after each applauds. He decided to go up into the balcony to see why the young lad continued to look up and never turn and bow when the crowd would applaud. He discovered, when he reached the balcony, that the young lad was focused on the master teacher and would not allow himself to be distracted by applaud from the crowd. We must keep our eyes and focus on the master and allow Him to keep us focused. He's a mighty leader.

18

The Why Question of Human Suffering

(Mark 8:22-33)

There is perhaps no other universal question than the question "why". Why does God allow suffering? Why do bad things happen to good people? Why does God allow bad things to happen to good people? We hear and see this question being asked and uttered by Jesus in the extremities of His own suffering, "My God, My God, "Why hast Thou forsaken Me." It is not a question we face everyday, but it is a question that virtually everyone will ask at some point in life. This question will come especially in the midst of a personal crisis, at the death of a loved one, or in the wider tragedies of life. When our lives have been shattered by a personal tragedy, is there an answer? Is there an explanation? Is there any place we can go to find an answer when it appears that hope, peace and joy have been taken from us? No matter how devastating tragedy and suffering can be, it is a part of the human experience. Life is composed of joy, sorrow, justice, and injustices. Suffering comes in many forms. Suffering is not only physical; suffering can be emotional and/or mental as well as physical. The movie, "The Passion of Christ" demonstrates that suffering is emotional, mental and physical. Many people who have seen the movie feel that it was too brutal, as to minimize the suffering of Jesus. The prophet Isaiah said, "He was wounded for our transgressions, bruised for our iniquities, and the chastisement of our peace was be upon Him. Surely He has bored our grief and carried our sorrow. He was despised and we esteemed Him not, smitten of God and afflicted" *(Isaiah 53:3-4)*. Suffering has no respecter of persons. *(Matthew 5:45)* says, "The lord allows His sun to shine on the just as well as the unjust, and His rain to fall on the just as well as the unjust." Suffering has no respecter of persons. The Apostle Paul tells us in *(Philippians 3:10)*, "That we are called to share in the fellowship of His sufferings." *(Roman 8:17)* says, "If we indeed suffer with Him, that we may also be glorified with Him." The major and minor prophets raised this question of suffering. Why is an ancient question. The prophet Habakkuk, the prophet Jeremiah, and the prophet Amos, all asked the question why. We are forever trying to find answers and make sense out of human suffering. Where is God when we are passing through sorrow that causes us to suffer? This is what Job asked when he was experiencing a series of tragedies in his life. "O that I may find Him and order my case." Many want to know where God is when they are suffering. Many people are quick to connect one's suffering with one's sin.

We can look back over our lives and see that some of the things we are suffering with or from are connected with some bad choices we have made, but not all suffering is due to one's sin. This was the position that Job's friends expressed to Job. They felt that Job was being punished because of some pass sin in his life. We do suffer sometimes because we have sinned but we do not suffer always because of our sin. *(2 Timothy 3:12)* says, "And all that would live Godly in Christ Jesus shall suffer persecution." So we do not always suffer for the wrong we have done, we suffer sometimes when we seek to live Godly for Christ. Jesus was obedient to the will of God but He suffered. *(Mark 8:31)* tells us that, "The Son of man would suffer many things." Suffering is difficult to handle whether we have caused it or God has allowed it. Suffering is inevitable; if we live long enough we will experience some form of suffering. There are different views about suffering. One view is that of simple physics, the physical laws are set into action. God watches, He observes from His position on the balcony of human affairs. There is nothing God can do to stop the physically inevitable. This view makes God powerless and not capable of helping us. The second view is God performs miracles for His people if they have faith in Him and call upon Him. If we don't have faith and call upon Him our problems don't turn out for our good. Even when we think we are living right, praying right and things do not turn out the way we prayed, then what? The third view is that God is sovereign, nothing happens outside the will and providence of God. The disadvantage of this view is that God appears to be inconsistent or God shows partiality. Why does God appear to help some people and neglect to hear or help others? How can we make sense seemingly of the inconsistency of God, as it relates to human suffering and evil? Joel Osteen had a young son dying of cancer. When someone would try to comfort or encourage him by affirming that God makes no mistakes, that nothing happens without it being His will, he said those affirming assurances would crumble, every time he knelt at his son's bed or saw him walk across the lawn noticing a limp. He would ask what the meaning of justice was if God was truly sovereign. Why do people die untimely deaths we ask? Why is there no discernible pattern in life and death? How do we answer the question of God's justice, His fairness, His involvement in the world as it relates to human affairs? Yes God is sovereign, He can do whatever He wants to do whenever He wants to do it, but that is not always comforting when a loved one has been taken away. Phillip Yancey, who wrote the book *"Disappointed with God"* said, "I have concluded that only God can determine what is of value to God." God resides in mystery; He is beyond our definition, He is beyond our rational. How then do we explain the mysteries and tragedies of life in human suffering?

I want to suggest a few explanations we can draw from. The **first thing** we must consider when a crisis or tragedy comes is that it serves to show exactly and precisely what kind of person we really are. It is so easy to live artificial and superficial lives convincing ourselves that we are all right. Nothing seems to shake us or disturb us at any level. But when a crisis or trial comes to test the very fiber of our faith, we seek a deeper sense in matters of our profession of faith. A crisis that causes us to suffer serves to demonstrate clearly what we really believe, and what the true nature of our faith is. Faith untested is not a genuine faith, it is only synthetic, and it's not real.

The **second perspective** of suffering I would like to suggest that we learn about God when it comes to human suffering is that God does not act impulsively. In Ravi Zacharias book, *"Jesus Among*

Other Gods," it says, "Is God the source of my suffering." It also states, "That God is the author and giver of life" and that life has a script that has been written. The prophet Jeremiah said that God has a plan for our lives. The script for our lives has been written. God knows the end from the beginning. Whatever happens in our lives works according to the purpose and counsel of His will. God does not impulsively or randomly pick on us. God does not treat us like some earthly potentate who delights in terrorizing us with undue suffering. God has ordered our steps from the beginning.

The **third perspective** I want to suggest that we learn about God in Human suffering is that God is never unjust in His dealings with us. (Psalm 103:10) says, "He, meaning God, has not dealt with us according to our sins, nor punished us according to our iniquities." Our sins deal with us more harshly than does God. Abraham said, "Shall not the judge of all the earth do right." God's judgment is always temperate with His mercy. It has been said that we are more punished by our sins than we are for our sins.

The **fourth perspective** I would like to suggest is that whatever happens that brings suffering has a purpose. God can and will use suffering and evil to fulfill His purpose. Joseph told his brothers in Genesis the fifth chapter, what they meant for evil for him God used it for good. God will never contradict Himself and His own purpose. God does not mislead us to cause us pain and suffering. He told His disciples in (St. John 16: 33), "In the world you will have tribulation, but be of good cheer, I have overcome the world." Whatever God's purpose is for your life maybe it be fulfilled. He that has begun a good work in you will complete the process until the day of Jesus Christ. We must remain steadfast and unshaken, being confident that ultimately all will be made plain and all will be well.

The **fifth and final perspective** I would like to suggest in understanding human suffering is that there are some things not meant for us to know, that some secrets belong to God. There are some things in life that deal with suffering and evil that remains a mystery. There are some things we will never know or understand. (Deuteronomy 29:29) says, "The secret things belong to the Lord our God, but those things that have been revealed belong to us and to our children forever, that we may do all the works of this law." A late lady friend of mine battled with cancer for six years and eventually surrendered to cancer and died. Prior to her death she asked me to give her a religious perspective of suffering and evil in the world. She had been through eight different cancer treatments but to no avail. The question as to why some people survive cancer and some don't was a question I could not answer rationally other than some people catch the cancer in time and it can be treated and cured, and some are not cured even if they catch it in time. The only answer or response I had was that some things we do not know and some questions we cannot answer. One thing I was concerned about during her sickness was if she had ever committed her life to Christ. Well a few hours before she died I prayed with her and heard her ask God to have mercy on her and save her. One thing I could not explain was why she could not get well, but what I do know is that she died in the Lord. "For we know that all things work together for the good of them that love the Lord and are called according to His purpose" *(Romans 8:28).* Only God knows why some people get sick and get well and others don't. Only God knows why all sickness is not unto death. Only God knows why the righteous have to suffer unjustly, only God knows why there are some things we cannot change. We know in part, but one day when the balance has been struck, we will know. One day we'll understand it better by and by. But until then we have to keep on trusting and believing that all mysteries will be revealed to us. When time shall be no more we will know as we are known. When the fog has been lifted we will know. When death has met it final foe we shall know.

19

Seven Signs of Being Born Again

(St John 3:1-21)

The call to discipleship is a mandate from God Himself. The German theologian, Dietrich Bonhoeffer, says when Christ calls a man, "He bids him to come and die." The Apostle Paul said, "I have been crucified with Christ, its no longer I who live but Christ lives in me; and the life which, I now live I live in the flesh I live by faith in the son of God who loved me and gave Himself for me" (Galatians 2:20). "I die daily," said Paul. Paul realized answering the call to follow Christ meant dying to self. Following Christ involves a crucifixion of self. Jesus said to Nicodemus, "You must be born again." You must die and be born again, have a new birth. A new birth must take place in your life. "Except a man is born again he cannot see the kingdom of God." The new birth involves a reorientation of life. A transformation of a person's life takes place. When a person becomes a Christian their life style is transformed. Their priorities change. When we are born again our schedules change. Our desires change, our values change, and our economics change. Some of our friendships change, and our view of the world and others change. There is a difference between the physical and the spiritual births. Jesus told Nicodemus that which is born of the flesh is flesh and that which is born of the spirit is spirit. The physical birth is not accomplished without a gestation period. The fetus does not participate in the developmental process. The time of the process of development of the fetus is predictable. The spiritual birth gestation period or process is sudden or indeterminate in length. Meaning the new birth of a person can take place anytime and any place. There is a fundamental difference between being born physically and being born spiritually. When we are born spiritually we play a role in the spiritual development process. We help determine if we grow or remain stagnant. When we talk about being born again we want to first begin by talking about what being born again is *not*. The Eastern Orthodox theologians approach the reason toward the being of God from the via negativa, meaning the way of the negatives by saying what something is not before we define what it is. Being born again is *not* thinking you are better than others because you do not do as others do. Being born again is *not* being self-righteous and looking down on others. Being born again is *not* just saying you believe in God. Believing in God is basic for being born again but it takes more than just believing. The demons believe and even tremble but they are still demons. Being born again is *not* supporting some social cause. Being born again is *not* just coming to church on Sunday. Being born again does *not* mean that because you support the church you are supposed to have your way or control the church, that's not being born again. Being a good person does *not* mean you are born again. Just because you have not robbed or killed anyone does not qualify you for being born again. Just because a person is basically a good person does not mean they are born again. I had a man tell me that people are inherently or innately good. We are all born and made in the image of God and there is some good in all of us. Everything God created or made was good. But when man broke fellowship with God in the Garden of Eden, the God in man left man. Man is inherently or innately good to a certain point. The term being born again is mentioned twice in the New Testament. (1 Peter1:23) says, "Born again not of the corruptible seed but of the incorruptible, by the word of God that liveth and abideth forever." And we have Jesus telling Nicodemus, a ruler of the Jews, that he must be born again. There are seven signs I feel that are indicators of the new birth.

The **first sign** of the new birth in a person's life is that person has a sense and knowledge of their sin. In the sixth chapter of Isaiah when Isaiah saw the Lord in the temple high and lifted up, he was convicted of his sin and said, "Woe is me, for I am a man of unclean lips." There is something wrong with a person's salvation and their profession of faith when they know they are sinning and are not willing to do anything about it. The Apostle Paul stated in *(Romans 6:1-2)*, "Shall we continue in sin that grace may abound? God forbid! How shall we, who died to sin, live any longer in sin?" When a person has truly been born again they do not practice sin; that is not to say that they will not sin. They live being mindful that they are sinful in the sense that brings destruction to themselves as well as others. What often happens when one does not have a sense of what is moral or spiritual, they find themselves saying and doing things that not only hurt them but also hurt others. There are many people and many being Christians that do things to one another, good or bad, and fail to realize that the things they do are things done unto God. What this says is that they will not become a slave to sin or allow sin to have dominion over them. A person who has been born again realizes that, "If we sin, we have an advocate with the Father, Jesus Christ the righteous: and he is the propitiation for our sins; and not for our sin only but for the sins of the whole world" *(John 2:1-2)*.

The **second sign** of the new birth is genuine repentance. Not only does a person have a sense of their sin, they are willing to do something about their sin. The Apostle Paul said in *(1 Corinthians11: 31)*, "If we would judge ourselves we would not be judged." God would not have to judge us if we would judge ourselves. The prodigal son said these words when he had fallen into sin, "I will arise and go to my father and say father I have sinned against heaven and before thee I am no longer worthy to be called thy son." He judged himself to be in sin and out of the will of God. He was willing to repent of his sin, meaning he was willing to turn from his sin and turn to God. Repentance means to make a complete turn in your life. It is to make a one hundred and eighty degree turnaround. When we have truly been born again we do not continue in sin and try to justify why we are sinning, we do something about it. We seek God's forgiveness. As the prodigal son's Father was waiting for him to return home, God is longsuffering toward us, not willing that any should perish but come to repentance.

The **third sign** of the new birth is that others who know us will notice a real change in us and can testify to the change. In (Acts, 4:13) it says, many of the people who knew Peter and John saw their boldness and knew that they were unlearned men but stated that they realized they had been with Jesus. When one has had an encounter with Christ as Paul and Peter had, others will be able to bear witness to the change or transformation. *(2 Corinthians 5:17)* says, "Therefore if any man be in Christ he is a new creation; old things are passed away behold all things become new." All things become new, not some things, but all things. We have a new walk, a new talk, a new peace, a new love, a new hope, and a new joy. The joy of the Lord is your strength. We have a peace that surpasses all understanding. We seek to walk worthy of our calling. We walk as children of light. All things become new, not some things, but all things become new. The apostle Paul said to the church in *(2Corinthians 3:2),* "Ye are our epistle written in our hearts, known and read by all men." When we are born again, people who are Christians as well as those that are not, read our lives.

The **fourth sign** of the new birth is one lives by their faith. The Apostle Paul stated in *(Galatians 2:20),* "I have been crucified with Christ, it is no longer I who live, but Christ lives in me; and the life I now live in the flesh I live by faith in the Son of God, who loved me and gave Himself for me." When we are born again we live by our faith. The just shall live by his faith. We walk by faith and not by sight. Therefore being justified by faith we have peace with God through our Lord Jesus Christ. To live by faith means that our faith is established according to the word of God. "Faith comes by hearing, and hearing by the word of God" *(Romans 10:17).* God has dealt to every man a measure of faith. Our faith gives us knowledge of the promises of God. Our faith enables us to believe that with God all things are possible to them that believe. Our faith enables us to call those things that are not, as though they were. This is what Abraham did, he said to Isaac, "That the Lord would provide." Our faith enables us to trust what we believe and know to be the truth. Our faith challenges us to obey God. Our faith challenges us to hope even when we cannot see what lies ahead of us. Faith says hope that is seen is not hope. Faith gives us substance to hope for.

The **fifth sign** of the new birth is consistency between one's life and one's confession. All too often people who say they are saved or born again say one thing but live contrary to their confession and profession. They act holy when they are in the church but when they get outside of the church their language and life style changes. Peter said to Jesus in His presence, "Lord I will die for you and even go to prison for you." He made a great profession in the presence of Jesus but when he left the presence of Jesus and was asked if he was one of His followers he changed immediately in the presence of others. A person who has been truly saved and has converted their lifestyle, as a Christian, will be consistent. The world is looking for men and women of God who are not ashamed or afraid to acknowledge that they are Christians, privately or publicly. Jesus said, "Whosoever therefore would be ashamed of me and my words in this adulterous and sinful generation; of him also shall the Son of man be ashamed, when he comes in the glory of his Father with the holy angles." In *(Mark 8:38)* Jesus said to Peter, "When you are converted strengthen your brother."

The **sixth sign** of the new birth is that one acknowledges that his or her life is under the authority of God. If your life is not under the authority of God you will have problems dealing with authority. *(Romans 13:1-2)* says, "Let every soul be subject to the governing authorities. For there is no authority except from God, and God appoints the authorities that exist." Therefore whoever resists the authority resists the ordinance of God, and those who resist will bring judgment on themselves." God has a plan for every Christian when it comes to submitting to authority. God's plan for spiritual authority in our lives is to protect our lives. Christians are to be law-abiding citizens in their communities, on their jobs and in the body of Christ. Whenever a person who says he or she is saved has a problem with following leadership, their salvation can be called into question. Before one can be set in authority, one has to first set under authority. Jesus said I must do the works of him that has sent me. Jesus acknowledged that he was under the authority of the Father.

The **seventh and final sign** of the new birth or being born again is an "attitude to serve." When Isaiah was saved and cleansed in the temple and the call to serve was issued, Isaiah said, "Here am I send me." When Paul was saved and repented of his sins Paul said to Jesus, "Lord what would thou have me to do?" When a person is truly born again they do not tell God what they are going to do and what they are not going to do. They will say Lord what will you have me to do. Many people who say they are Christians are like Jonah; they tell God no by their actions. And when you go against God the judgment of God will come upon you. When it comes to being a servant of God, it is not about a position, or about one's degree or degrees, it's about being used by God. In the words of the late Dr. Martin Luther King, "Anybody can be great because anybody can serve. You don't need a degree to serve. You don't have to make your subject and verb agree to serve. You don't need to know Einstein's Theory of Relativity to serve, or know about Plato and Aristotle to serve. You don't have to know the second theory of thermo-dynamics to serve. You only need a heart full of grace. A soul generated by love." We are saved to serve. Saved to live for Christ; saved to serve this present age. Saved to the uttermost; to the uttermost Jesus saves, He will pick you up and turn you around; Jesus saves!

20

Allowing God to Use What We Have

(2 Corinthians 8:7-19)

There is an irony as it relates to the ways of God. God does not see things nor does He do things the way you and I would do them. Our perception of life or things varies, unlike God. Although perception is not always reality, for some people it is reality. If we were to look at a glass of water that was not completely full some would see it from two different perspectives. Some would see it half full and others would see it half empty. How we view, or evaluate some things will determine how we respond. People are more governed by the things they have no control of rather than the things they have control of. Over the length and breath of my ministry I have heard and seen people talk about what they could not do based on what they do not have rather than what they have. "We can't do this or that because it isn't but a few of us." I had a man, who was once a member of my Church, say to me before he left, "I don't think you have enough people now to build or buy a church;" such withering words and comments. For a while, I was impacted by his words because it appeared that those that remained were so indecisive and uncommitted that it seemed as though his words were true. But when it comes to the work of God we cannot always be wearied by what people say.

I recently watched a documentary on the Oakland Raiders. I heard Al Davis, the owner; say if you allow what people say to determine what you do or how you think you will not go very far in life. We come to our text where we hear the Apostle Paul appealing to the church at Corinth to give generously to the mother church. The Jerusalem church being the mother church was poor. Paul wanted all the Gentile churches to remember and help in the support the mother church. Paul was encouraging them to give for two reasons. He did not command them to give. He encouraged them to give. Paul encouraged them to give because it would be a good example for them as Christians. Secondly, he encouraged them to give because it would prove their sincerity and love for others. We are not only to love in Word but in deed also. Paul goes on to talk about how Jesus gave of Himself for us. "For we know the grace of our Lord Jesus Christ, that though He was rich, yet for your sakes He became poor, that you through His poverty might be rich."

The Corinthians had made a pledge to support the mother church but had failed to live up to their pledge. Paul was telling them that they should live up to the pledge they had made. People make pledges or promises and do not live up to them. People join the church and sign the church covenant but will not live up to the covenant. God does not ask us to do anything we are not able to do. God wants only a portion of that which we already have. God only requires us to give a portion of that which He has already blessed and provided for us. Listen to our text; "For if there first be a willing mind, it is accepted according to that a man hath, and not according to that he hath not." God does not expect us to give what we do not have but only a portion of that which we have. "For if there first be, a willing mind." The mind is the Master power that molds and makes, and man is mind, he takes the tools of thoughts, and shapes what he wills. The bible talks about the mind and the will as it relates to man. (Proverbs 23:7) says, "As a man thinks in his heart so is he." (Romans 12:1) says, "Be transformed by the renewing of your mind." (Philippians 2:5) says, "Let this mind be in you, which was also in Christ Jesus." The reason many people do not go very far in life is because they lack the will. They tell themselves and allow others to tell them that they cannot achieve. The late Dr. Benjamin Elijah Mays, when asked how he achieved so much in life, said people would tell him, "Bennie you are going to be somebody." He went on to say that if they said he could do it, he believed he could do it. So we heard Paul telling the Corinthians when it comes to giving and doing the work of the church that it starts first with the *Will* and the *Mind*. The Greek word for "mind" is nous. When the apostle Paul told the church at Philippi to let this mind be in you that was also in Christ Jesus, what he was encouraging them to do was to position their mind where Christ's mind was, to have the mind of Christ. One's ability to achieve starts with how one thinks. As a man thinks, so is he.

The first thing we want to look at when it comes to doing the work of God is; is there a willing mind. God is not going to force His will on us. In (*John 5:6*) Jesus said to the man who had an infirmity for thirty-eight years, "Wilt thou be made whole." What we will is equally as important as what God wills. When Nehemiah was rebuilding the walls of

Jerusalem and he met much opposition in rebuilding the walls, the scripture tells us in (*Nehemiah 4:6*), "That the people had a mind to work." If first there be a willing mind.

The **second thing** we must notice and understand when it comes to doing the work of God is that, God only uses that which we have. If first there be a willing mind, it is accepted according to that a man hath, not according to what he hath not. If you always look at what you do not have you will never do anything. When Jesus asked the Disciples what they had to feed the five thousand, they said there was a Lad with five barley loaves and two fish: and one of them said what are they among so many? So often we are quick to devalue that which we already have. Jesus did not ask them what they did not have; He asked them what they had. God only wants to use what we have. He took five barley loaves and two fish and fed five thousand. Little becomes much when you are willing to put it in God's hands. All God wants us to do is offer to Him that which we have. If we are willing to offer to God what we have, it will be accepted. When the farmers in Tuskegee, Alabama were told they had to abandon their farms and move west because the land would not grow anything but sweet potatoes and peanuts, Dr. Carver went to work. He was willing to use what he had, in spite of, and developed one hundred and fifty products from peanuts and three hundred products from potatoes. Dr. George Washington Carver first had a willing mind. He was willing to use what he had. If first there be a willing mind it is accepted according to what one has.

The **third thing** we must do with what we have is, offer what we have to God. Whatever we have, whether it is great or small, God has given it to us. Whatever God has given, He expects us to offer it back to him. I remember when I got out of the service in 1983 and finished undergraduate studies at Clark-Atlanta University and applied for seminary, I felt that I had much to offer but I knew that God had called *me to* the Christian ministry. I was reluctant at first to go to seminary but I spoke with Dean Randle Ruble at Erskine Theological Seminary in Due West, South Carolina and he encouraged me to come and offer God what I had. I have discovered over the years that if we offer God what we have that which seems to be nothing, becomes something, and that which appears to be insufficient becomes sufficient. God can open doors that no man can open and shut doors no man can open.

The **fourth and final thing** it takes for God to use what we have to do the work of God is faith. A working faith, "faith without works is dead." We must have the will to believe, the will to trust, and the will to work. "If thou can just believe all things are possible." Things with man are impossible but with God all things are possible to them that believe. According to your faith be it done unto you. Without faith it is impossible to please God, for he that would come to him must believe that he is a rewarder to them that diligently seek him. (Hebrew 11:6). By faith Abraham, when he was called to go out into a place, which he should after receive for an inheritance, obeying; and he went out, not knowing whither he went. "By faith Moses, when he had come to years refused to be called the son of Pharaoh's daughter, chose to suffer affliction with the people of God than to enjoy the pleasures of sin for a season. By faith the harlot Ra'hab perished not with them that believed not, when she had received the spies. By faith the walls of Jericho fell down, after they were compassed about seven days.

21

When Jesus Shows Up

(St. John 20:19-29)

The death and resurrection of Jesus was met with doubt, disbelief, sorrow, feelings of hopelessness and powerlessness. There were some who felt disillusioned by the death of Jesus. In Luke's account there were two men on the Emmaus road who said to Jesus not knowing it was Him, "That we had hoped He would be the one to redeem Israel." We see that the death and resurrection was shrouded and mixed with emotions of sorrow and disappointment. Life is a continual series of beginnings and endings. And from the beginning and ending of life we are marked and tailored for certain trials. We see this in our country with two prominent families, to mention a few, marked by tragedy. The Kennedy Family and the King Family both have been marked by tragedy. Some people have said that the Kennedy family's series of tragedies have come because of their sins. We do suffer because of our sin but suffering is not always related to one's sin. Jesus refuted this hypothesis in the ninth chapter of John's gospel. The question was asked to Jesus concerning the man born blind, "Who sinned, this man or his parents?" Jesus said, "Neither did this man sin or his parents but that the works of God should be revealed in him." What this statement says in this instance is God had a greater purpose for this man. God can use whatever happens in our lives and fulfill a greater purpose He has for us. Jesus suffered and He did not sin. God works according to the counsel and purpose of His will. In our text we come to one of the post resurrection appearances of Jesus. Jesus made known His presence on many occasions after His death. Even though He told them that after three days He would rise, they were slow to believe. We are slow to believe God because we cannot see beyond our circumstances and this creates disbelief. Faith is acting on what we believe not because we can see it but because we believe. Believing is seeing. All too often we say we believe but we fail to practice what we believe. God does not force us to believe, He tells us, "If thou can just believe all things are possible." What we see Jesus doing after His resurrection and before His ascension is verifying His resurrection in a number of post resurrection appearances. Jesus as the Son of God and Son of man was a man of truth and integrity. His post resurrection appearances served to confirm the truth about His death and resurrection. Even though He presented Himself alive by many infallible proofs, there were still some who doubted and did not believe.

Thomas, one of the disciples of Jesus doubted. When Jesus first appeared unto His disciples in the upper room Thomas was not present. Thomas is an example of what happens when one in leadership is out of place. He demonstrates to us that when you are out of place you cannot know what is going on and what is being done. This is what happens so often in the church, persons who are in a position of leadership are often out of place. Thomas was one of the disciples whom Jesus would give an apostolic commission needed to witness the resurrection of Jesus if he was to go forth in the apostolic succession. The apostles would establish the church, not build the church. We must remember that we are only apart of God's network. The church does not live because people live; the church lives because Christ lives. When death, sorrow, fear, disbelief and doubt come upon us what does Jesus do to reassure us that He lives?

The **first thing** He does is makes known His presence. Our text tells us that the doors were shut where the disciples were assembled because they were afraid of the Jews. When we are gripped by fear, sorrow, disbelief and doubt we often shut the doors of our heart and mind. Jesus meets us where we are regardless of our state of mind or state of being. He came among them and was in their midst and made His presence known. There is such a ministry known as the ministry of presence. Jesus was instilling in His disciples in the garden of Gethsemane. He said to them, "Could you not sit with me one hour?" He needed their presence and companionship in His final hours. Being present does not mean that we can change anything. So He made known His presence to them when they needed to be reassured that all was not lost. When I was a hospital chaplain at Athens Regional Medical Center in Georgia, one evening I made a pre-surgical visit to a patient's room and discovered that the lady who was to undergo surgery the following morning was gripped with anxiety and fear. It was her first time in the hospital and the first time she would have major surgery. Her request to me was, would I go with her into the operating room and hold her hand while she prepared for surgery, because she did not want to be left alone. Our presence with those in fear helps to relieve their fears. (Isaiah 43:2) says, "When thou passest through the waters, I will be with thee; and through the rivers, they shall not overflow thee: when thou walkest through the fire, thou shalt not be burned; neither shall the flame kindle upon thee." Whenever and wherever we need the presence of God, He is there.

The **second thing** He does when He shows up is give us His peace. He said to them, "Peace be unto you." He gives us peace with God, peace from God and the peace of God. The peace of God means we can trust God because we are in the right relationship with God. "Therefore being justified by faith we have peace with God" *(Romans 5:1)*. When we are at peace with God then we have peace from God, and having peace from God gives us the peace of God that surpasses all understanding. My late lady friend was told that she was going to die after battling breast cancer for over six years. When I went to her hospital room to visit, she informed me that her doctor had stated that she going to die and her death was imminent. She told me she did not want to die, but she was at peace and things were no longer in her hands but God's hands. She was at peace with God and had peace from God and the peace of God. When Jesus shows up He gives us His peace and allows us to face life and the challenges life brings to each of us.

The **third thing** He gives us when He shows up is Proof of His presence and peace. The text says, "He showed them His hands and His side." God does not mislead us or deceive us as to who He is and what He will do. *(Psalm 119:89)* says, "Forever O Lord thy word is settled in heaven. The Lord watches over His word to perform it." God is not a man that He should lie, or the Son of man that He should repent. God's word is truth and God does not have to retract anything that He has said. He will not go back on His word. So He showed them His hands and His side as evidence of His crucifixion and death. He showed them His hands and side in a bodily form as the resurrected Christ. He shows up in many cases and places we would least expect. His word assures us that because He lives we can live also. Thomas said that he would not believe except he saw the nail prints in His hands and where they pierced Him in His side. Well Jesus showed up and said to Thomas, "Reach hither thy finger, and behold My hands, and reach hither thy hand, and thrust it into My side: and be not a faithless, but believing" *(John 20:27).*

The **fourth thing** He does when He shows up is give us purpose and direction. He says, in our text, "As the Father has sent Me, I also send you." Jesus had fulfilled His purpose when on the cross He uttered, "It is finished." He had redeemed man from the curse of the law. He had paid the penalty for our sin. He had settled the old account and made a way for man to come back to God. He tells them, "As the Father has sent Me, I also send you." Every Christian has a God given purpose while they are here. We are first created to worship Him. Our purpose is found in the word of God. The reason so many men and women are unhappy and unfulfilled is because their lives lack purpose and direction. Many are not aware of God's purpose for their lives. I was talking with a young man once and I saw that he had a book and I asked him what was he reading? The book he was reading dealt with real estate - how to be a millionaire. He stated that this is what it's all about. I said to him success is not measured in money and things. They are a part of life but life is not all about money and things. Prosperity is a part of God's plan and purpose for our lives. The bible teaches that, "A man's life consisted not of the abundance he possesses." We should not allow the things that we acquire to define who we are, but we should be defined by what we deposit in the earth that will bless and benefit others. God has a greater purpose for our lives. We need to seek first the kingdom of God and all of his righteousness and all these things shall be added. Everything we have need of is in the kingdom if we seek first the kingdom.

The **fifth thing** Jesus gives us when He shows up is power to go forth and fulfill our purpose. Our text says, He said to them, "Receive ye the Holy Ghost." In the first chapter of the book of (Acts 1:8), He told them that, "Ye shall receive power after the Holy Spirit comes upon you and you shall be witnesses unto Me." The Christian is never without power unless he or she is disconnected from the power source. Spiritual power comes through fasting and prayer. Our power comes by way of trials and infirmity. Paul had an infirmity, a thorn in his flesh, but God told him His grace was sufficient. And God told him that he was given a thorn that the power of God may rest upon him. Isaiah forty says, "He gives power to the faint, not to the strong and to them that have no strength he increases their might." Ah my brother, ah my sister if we want power we have to face our trials with faith in God. A legendary preacher named James Stewart was asked, "Who taught you to sing?" His reply, "Sorrow." "Who taught you to pray?" His reply was, "Problems." He stated, "For when problems came there was nowhere for me to go but to my knees." It takes heartache and heartbreak but God is taking out of us only to pour into us. The Holy Spirit gives us power to overcome our trials and temptation. God helps us to turn our pain into power. There is power, wonder-working power, in the precious blood of the lamb.

The **sixth and final thing** that He gives us is His promise. "Lo," said Jesus, "I will be with you always, even unto the end of the age." He did not say I will be with you until, but He said unto the end. David said, "Yea though I walk through the valley and shadow of death I will fear no evil for thou art with me." God has promised to never leave us nor forsake us, and I believe the promise. God has promised when thou pass through the waters I will be with you and I believe the promise. God has promised to supply all our needs according to His riches in glory through Christ Jesus and I believe the promise. God has promised when we stand between the living and the dead to stay the course and I believe the promise. God has promised if we are faithful over a few things He would make us ruler over many things and I believe the promise. I've seen the lighting flashing, I've heard the thunder roar, I've felt sin breakers dashing trying to conqueror my soul, but I've heard the voice of Jesus telling me to still fight on. He's promised never to leave me, never to leave me alone.

22

When You Want To Quit

(1Kings 19:1-18)

There are some things we deal with on a daily bases that have a tendency to drain us, exhaust us, deplete us, frustrate us, weary us and leave us empty. However, in the service of God, God allows us to grow weary, frustrated, but He does not accept quitting or giving up. The scriptures encourage each of us to endure hardness, as a good soldier of Jesus Christ. "Be thou faithful unto death, and I will give you a crown." Sometimes there appears to be no spiritual vitality or power available to us. We become burned out and sometimes we are driven to despair, and depression sets in. We are pressed beyond measure. We become faint hearted if we don't faint first.

We come now to the prophet Elijah who fits the description of the vicissitudes that we go through in life. God had used the prophet Elijah in a mighty way. Elijah himself is not a prophet but a prophecy. His experience is for our instruction. Elijah is a prophet we can all identify with in many ways. We, like Elijah, enter into strange and mysterious states of depression ourselves. Weary, and sick at heart, sorely tried and apt to faint. Our tendency to faint is not a strange thing that happens; it's a part of life. In looking down through the sands of time we see footprints of men and women who have been subjected to depression, oppression and resignation with life. Elijah was a man of like passions with us. He failed in the point wherein he was strongest, as many other saints have; Abraham, Job, Moses, David and Peter to mention a few. He suffered from rash reaction. He was wearied by excitement. He wished for folly; "O Lord take my life," was his cry. He fled from death, because if he had really wanted to die all he had to do was run to Jezebel instead of fleeing from her to save his life. He became exhausted running from Jezebel.

Sometimes we wear ourselves out, and burn ourselves out by running from things instead of dealing with them. We probably would spend less energy if we confronted the problem instead of fleeing from the problem. When we are afraid, tired, and stressed out we have a tendency to overreact or act irrationally. We, like Elijah, think we are the only ones having a hard time sometimes. We think sometimes we are the only one who is on the Lord's side or working for the Lord. Here was a prophet who had slain the prophets of Baal. False worship had been dismantled. Israel had moved into the Kingdom of God. But in a single moment or day these bright achievements had been clouded. Elijah allowed a threat from Jezebel to overwhelm him to the point that he was driven to despair. Here was the prophet of God fainting and wanting to give up on life and God. He was dispirited; his spirit was dejected and prostrate. He was a prophet who could raise the dead, open and shut the heavens; summon fire and water with his prayers. He had killed four hundred and fifty Baalites with the sword. But now we see this prophet shrinking at the frowns and threats of a woman, Jezebel. So we hear this prophet saying, "It's enough, I have had it, no more of this nonsense. I would rather die than live." Well the best of us, the strongest and holiest saints have wanted to succumb to death as a way out of our depression or distress. I too have seen periods or times in my life when I prayed for death. There have been times when it did not matter to me whether I lived or died. Well what we think is enough may not be enough for God. God has so much to teach us before He can use us in a greater way; it is up to Him to say when enough is enough. God rejuvenated Elijah and gave him the gift of sleep, rest. Normally when a person is depressed and emotionally drained it takes sleep a long time to come. God gave Elijah rest from his depression and frustration. A good night's rest can make a big difference in how you look at a situation. When we are tired, depressed and frustrated we are very vulnerable. This was the case with Elijah.

Sleep is sometimes better than medicine. Not only did God give him rest, He gave him a meal. He gave him some sustenance for his body and water to quench his thirst. Then, He revealed Himself and His ways to Elijah. He calmed his stormy mind by the healing influences of nature. He commanded the hurricane to sweep the sky, and the earthquake to shake the ground. He lit up the heavens till they were one mass of fire. When we know what God can do and where God is we are less troubled about extraneous matters. Often we allow things that are extraneous, outside us, to bedevil us. When the Disciples on the Sea of Galilee were able to wake up Jesus and were sure that Jesus cared, their fears were removed.

Well, what should we do when we want to quit? What can we do when we are overwhelmed by fear?

The Psalmist David said, "When my heart is overwhelmed lead me to the rock that's higher than I."

The **first thing** that most of us need when we want to quit is to get some rest. We need physical rest, emotional rest, and mental rest. We need to learn to rest in the Lord, rest in His Word. (*Psalm 37:7*) says, "Rest in the Lord and wait patiently for Him, feed on His faithfulness and verily thou shall be fed." In the fourth and fifth verse of our text we see that Elijah came to a juniper tree and requesting of the Lord to die, laid down and went to sleep. Sometimes a good night's rest can serve to help us look at things from a different perspective when we have had some time to clear our mind. After Elijah was able to rest, he rose up and went in renewed strength the next day to face the journey. That's why Jesus said, "Come unto Me, all ye that labor and are heavy laden and I will give you rest, take My yoke upon you and learn of Me, and ye shall find rest unto your souls, For My yoke is easy and My burden is light" (Matthew11:28-30). We must seek God more when we feel panic stricken and we want to give up.

The **second thing** we need to do when we want to quit is, after we have gotten some rest, reassess the situation. In verse 5 of the nineteenth chapter of I Kings, the Angel of the Lord touched Elijah and said unto him, "Arise." When one rises after a good night's sleep, things around us will look different. The load feels lighter and the day can look a little brighter. The angel spoke to Elijah and told him not only to arise, but also to eat. We are mortal and our bodies have to be replenished physically. God had provided the sustenance his body needed to face what lay ahead of him.

We will never know God's renewing power if we fail to stand up and look up. While we are assessing our situation count your blessings. Sometimes all people need is to be told to stand up. Jesus told many, whom He healed, to get up. He did not have to touch them; He just told them to get up. Jesus instructed one man to get up and take up his bed and walk. We need to get up and stand in the power of His might. I remember back in 1989, I had not finished seminary and I was lacking one year from completing my Masters of Divinity. Feeling low, I called my former Clinical C.P.E. Supervisor. He asked me if I had finished my work yet and I stated no. I went on to say to him that I was in a situation and I did not have anyone to help me financially go back to school. His reply to me was not what I expected. He stated to me that I needed to get up and make it happen. When he told me to get up, I got up and with the help of God we made it happen. I got up, went over to Samford University in Birmingham, Alabama and discovered the University had a School of Divinity called Beeson Divinity School. I also learned that they had grants available for students who wanted to attend or finish seminary. It did not happen for me until I was told to get up and I responded. God will send people to us who know what to say to us when we are at wits end.

The **third thing** we must do when we want to quit is look up. The Psalmist David said, "I will lift up mine eyes unto the hills from whence cometh my help, my help cometh from the Lord" (Psalm 121). In the book of Revelation, the fourth chapter, verse 1, it says, "Come up hither, and I will show thee things which must be hereafter." When we look up, God will show us things that we have never seen or imagined could happen for us. When we look up, we can see that dark clouds have passed over. When we look up, God shows us a shaft of light to let us know that there is still hope. Whenever we look up, things will begin to look up. The story is told about a mother and her son who were getting ready to go to Church one Sunday morning. But on this particular morning the mother decided she was not going to church, she was sending her son. The little boy said to his mother, "Mama, what's wrong?" The mother replied, "I'm tired this morning. I don't know how I'm going to pay the rent this month. Your dad has blown his money gambling again; I've had enough." The little boy said to his mother, "Mama, did you tell me God is able? You always told me to look up when things were going wrong; look up mama, God is able." When we look up things will change. When we look and keep looking up things have a way of coming together. We must put our eyes upon the God of our Salvation. In (2 Chronicles 20:12) Je-hosh-a-phat says, "Neither know we what to do: but our eyes are upon Thee." We must keep our eyes upon Jesus, and look unto Him the author and finisher of our faith.

The **fourth thing** we must do when we want to quit is, hook up to the power source. 1 Kings, verse 11 of the nineteenth chapter says that Elijah went and stood upon Mount Horeb before the Lord. How do we connect with our power source? How do we become renewed when we are exhausted? When we are overwhelmed with fear, where do we find power and strength for the journey? Well, we have to know how to access God's power and strength and that is we go to the Word of God to renew our strength. I remember years ago I was in seminary and I wanted to quit. I was exhausted; I wanted to give in to my exhaustion and quit. I had exams to take, research papers due and no strength or motivation; I was mentally, emotionally, physically, and spiritually drained. I went to (*Isaiah 40 verses 29-3*) where it says, "He the Everlasting God, the Lord, the Creator, fainteth not, neither is weary; there is no searching of His understanding. He giveth power to the faint; and to them that have no might He increaseth their strength." I read these verses that promised renewal. Then I remembered what (*Luke 18:1*) said, "Men ought to always pray and faint not." Then I went down on my knees and prayed, I remember that He said, "He giveth power to the faint; and to them that have no might He increaseth their strength." God has promised to renew our strength. David said, "I would have fainted unless I believed I would see the goodness of the Lord in the land of the living." I prayed fervently and reminded God what He had promised when my strength and might was gone. I reminded Him that He said, He would renew my strength. I reminded Him that He said He would never leave me nor forsake me. I reminded Him that He said that He was the saving strength of His anointed. I reminded Him that He had promised if I grow not weary in well doing, I would reap the harvest. When I finished praying, my strength was renewed like the eagle. I was able to mount up with renewed vigor and vitality and with a new peace, a new determination, a new hope, a new commitment and a new power.

Wait on the Lord, wait I say on the Lord.

23

Whose Side Are You On?

(Exodus 32:15-29)

In the moral and spiritual realm there are two contending forces, the kingdom of God and the kingdoms of this world. There can be no neutrality, straddling or middle ground when it comes to serving God. The moral realm says we are to do what's morally right, but a moral person is not necessarily a spiritual person. However, when a person has been born of the spirit of God, a spiritual person is suppose to be a moral person. A spiritual person does what is right because God is a God of righteousness and justice. The spirit of God leads and directs a spiritual person. There comes a time in one's life when they will have to decide whose side they are on or where they stand. Jesus said, "Either you are with Me or against Me."

Many people say they are on the Lord's side but their lives or lifestyle does not bear witness as to whose side they are on. I read an article in Essence magazine in 2000. The question was asked to Denzel Washington, if his father, who was a minister, passed his religious roots down to his children. Denzel replied that there was no question about that. He went on to say that there comes a time when one has to decide whether they are going to stand for evil or good. Denzel stated that he stands for good. He went on to say, that, "I am not saying that I am anybody's saint, but I'm trying." He further said that he had decided where he was going to stand. He said as for me, "I'm standing on the side of God." This is the question that many people need to ask themselves in the world today, and some being Christians. Whose side are you on? Our text gives us an experience in the life of the children of Israel; Moses had gone to Mt. Sinai to receive the Ten Commandments and the instructions to build the tabernacle. While Moses was gone (hearing from God), Aaron allowed the people to get into liberalism and idolatry. One would have thought that Aaron, being a high Priest, would have stopped the people, but instead he went along with them. Aaron could not restrain the people while Moses was gone and he gave into their wishes. Where there is no vision the people are unrestrained. Aaron failed to give the people a vision of God. Aaron really had no true vision of God himself. Aaron allowed the people to tell him that Moses had deserted them. Their complaint was, "We do not know what has become of Moses." The people said this to Aaron, "Come make us gods that shall go before us."

The text says they took the gold earrings from among them and made a golden calf to worship. During that time, wearing earrings was a sign of idolatry and they brought this idea from Egypt with them. Aaron built an altar and made a proclamation and said, "Tomorrow is a feast to the Lord." How shaky can a leader be? The people did not want a leader that would follow God; they wanted a leader that they could tell what to do. People can steer the ship, but only the leader can chart the course. Aaron was willing to give into the wishes of the people instead of upholding Moses in his absence. They rose up early on the next day, offered burnt offerings, and brought peace offerings: and the people sat down to eat and drink, and rose up to play. God spoke to Moses while he was at Mt. Sinai and instructed him to go down because the people had corrupted themselves while he was gone. God went on to tell Moses that the people had turned quickly from the way that He had commanded them. It does not take long for people to stray or turn from God if they are not rooted and grounded in Him. When Moses came down from the mountain and saw the predicament the people were in, he asked them a pertinent question. Moses stood in the entrance of the camp and asked, "Who is on the Lord's side come to me." There is so much that is going on in our world today and in our churches that it is necessary that the people of God make a stand and say whose side they are on. One of our presidents once stated that he was on the Lord's side because he was a man of faith. One can have faith and not be on the Lord's side. Everything we do and believe is not of God. But what does matter is what we portray before the world regarding our conduct - how we treat one another, especially those who are different from us.

First, I want tell you what being on the Lord's side is not. Doing what is popular does not mean you are on the Lord's side. Popular can be wrong. Comprising the right for the wrong is not being on the Lord's side. Listening to what others have to say instead of seeking and listening to God is not being on the Lord's side. Influencing others to do what you would have them to do instead of telling them to follow God is not being on the Lord's side. Quitting on God when things do not go your way is not being on the Lord's side. Jesus said to the Father, "Not as I will but thy will be done." Being a lukewarm Christian is not being on the Lord's side. Advancing your cause instead of the cause of the kingdom is not being on the Lord's side. Robbing God of what belongs to Him, such as His tithes and offering, is not being on the Lord's side. Following others instead of following Christ is not being on the Lord's side. Sowing discord among the body of Christ is not being on the Lord's side. Blessed are the peacemakers for they shall be called the children of God. Now that we have an idea of what being on the Lord's side is not, we will look at what being on the Lord's side involves.

The **first thing** we want to notice that puts us on the side of God is following the leadership God has ordained for us to be under. God has placed every Christian under some leadership or authority. God, throughout the bible, has always worked through man to carry out His plan. The Levites were willing to respond to Moses' word from the Lord. They were willing to follow Moses' instructions from God. The apostle Paul said to the church at Corinth, "Follow me as I follow Christ." The children of Israel were not willing to follow Moses and his leadership. Therefore they were not on the Lord's side. (Romans13:1-2) says, "Let every soul be subject to the higher authority, for there is no authority except from God, and the authorities that exist are appointed by God." The children of Israel did not want to come under Moses' authority or leadership.

The **second thing** we notice that speaks to being on the Lord's side is a willingness to remove sin from our lives. The sword meant that they were to remove anyone or anything in their lives that was not on the Lord's side. If we are not careful, we will allow ourselves to get involved with family and friends whose lives demonstrate that they are not on the Lord's side. The Apostle Paul said, "Do not let sin reign in your mortal bodies." Sin robs us of those things that God would have enrich our lives with such as peace, joy happiness, health and wealth. Jesus said, "The thief comes to kill, to steal, and to destroy, but I am come that they might have life and have it more abundantly" *(John 10:10)*. The thief of jealousy, the thief of envy, the thief of greed, the thief of doubt, the thief of ungodly counsel, the thief of unbelief and the thief of deception; all of these things are against God because they are not of God. The wages of sin is death but the gift of God is eternal life through Jesus Christ our Lord" (Romans 6:23).

The **third thing** that the Levites did to show that they were on the Lord's side was consecrate themselves. Moses said to them in Exodus, chapter 32, verse twenty-nine, "Consecrate yourselves today to the Lord that He may bestow on you a blessing this day, for every man opposed his son and his brother." People who are on the Lord's side are consecrated to God and His work. They set themselves apart through prayer and study. They seek God and His will on a daily basis. The things of God are important to them and they desire to give God their best. To be consecrated means, to be prepared, to sanctify one's self for the Lord, and to purify oneself and to keep oneself holy unto the Lord. If we are going to be on the Lord's side we must purify our thoughts, our minds and our hearts. We must seek God daily. We must be in the world but not of the world.

The **fourth thing** that says one is on the Lord's

side is that they will not compromise what they believe. They will not bow down and serve any other God. In Daniel, the third chapter, we hear Shadrach, Meshach, and Abednego say to King Nebuchadnezzar, "If it be so, our God whom we serve is able to deliver us from the burning furnace; he will deliver us out of thine hand, O king. But if not, be it known unto thee, O king that we will not serve thy gods, nor worship the golden image which thou hast set up." They would not compromise what they believed. They would not denounce their faith and bow down and petition any other god but their God. A faith that will not compromise in the face of persecution is the God kind of faith. The young girl at Columbine High School in Colorado would not compromise what she believed in the face of death, because she knew in what she believed and who she believed and was not willing to compromise even if it meant she had to loose her life. "It has been said that if we will not stand for something we will fall for anything." We must stand when we have done all to stand, stand. The late Bishop Reuben Speaks would say, "If we are right, God will fight our battle."

The **fifth thing** that demonstrates that one is on the Lord's side is how they treat others. Jesus said the things we do to one another are things done unto Him. When we fail to visit the sick, the prisoner, clothe the naked, and feed the hungry we have done it unto Him. Jesus said, "Inasmuch as you have done it unto the least of these my brethren, you have done it unto me." We are called to labor together with God, not against Him, but with Him. The story is told about a young abbot who was working with a priest. There was a knock at the door one evening and when the young abbot answered the door he discovered it was a beggar. The beggar requested to speak with the priest but the young abbot stated to the beggar that the father was busy to come back later. The beggar left and came back later but the Father was still busy in his study. The Father heard the beggar at the door. He got up and went to the door but the young abbot said, "Father I told him you were still busy to come back later." The priest told the young abbot to let the beggar in, but the young abbot said to the priest, "You are leaving God." The priest said to the young abbot, "I am leaving God for God. We are our brother's keeper. We are His workmanship created in Christ Jesus for good works."

The **sixth and final thing** that demonstrates being on the Lord's side is making a public confession. Jesus said, "If ye be ashamed of Me in this sinful and adulterous generation I will be ashamed of you before My father in heaven." We cannot be ashamed to let others know that we are Christians. We are called to be witnesses unto Him. Joshua told whose side he and his family were on when he said, "As for me and my house, we will serve the Lord." David told whose side he was on when he said, "The Lord is my Shepard, I shall not want. He makes me to lie down in green pastures." The Apostle Paul told whose side he was on when he said, "For me to live is Christ and to die is gain." Paul told whose side he was on when he said, "I'm not ashamed of the gospel, for it is the power of God unto salvation to them that believe." Whose side are you on? Let the redeemed of the Lord say so. If you are a witness let God abide, if you have been converted let God abide. The world will know whose side we are on if we stand up for Jesus and confess Him as Lord and Savior.

24

Christmas, a Time to Worship

(Matthew 2:1-12)

The first "greatest event" in the life of Jesus is His conception and His birth. His conception was unusual, unnatural, supernatural and phenomenal. The first event is His Birth, His beginning. Jesus had His beginning outside of time. Eternity got into time and at the appointed time the Virgin Mary conceived and gave birth to the Christ child. The Prophets foretold of his Birth and His Birthplace. His coming was not a surprise; it was ordained from the foundation of the world. When He came, He had a purpose and mission to fulfill. His purpose was to seek and save that which was lost and to die and save us from our sins. He came to fulfill not His will but the Father's will. *(Hebrews 10:7)* says, "Then said I, Lo, I have come (in the volume of the book it is written of Me) to do thy will, O God." The heart of the Christmas story is that when we could not go to Him, He came to us. He did not have to come to us, but, "God so loved the world that He gave His only begotten Son." God commended His love toward us unconditionally. The birth of Jesus met the forces of opposition. His own mother and father questioned His conception. When it was time for Him to be born there was no room in the Inn. He had to be born in a stable. After He was born there was hostility and jealously by a king name Herod.

Many of the religious leaders knew about the birth of Jesus but they acted as if it had no significant meaning. They knew the truth; they knew where He would be born but did not show any interest or excitement. The only time they bore witness to the truth was when Herod heard about one being King of the Jews. The wise men came from the west to the east following the Star. The religious leaders of that day, as well as now, devalued, discounted the birth of Jesus. Many people in the church as well as outside the church misplace the value of His birth. Some place more significance on the tree than they do the Savior.

There are some issues in this country that seek to devalue Christmas. One of the issues in our country that seeks to under mind Christmas is that there are no movies about Christmas. The second issue is that they don't want us to say Merry Christmas; they want us to say happy holidays. The third issue is that they don't want Christmas carols being sung in neighborhoods. And the fourth issue is that certain businesses will not allow the Salvation Army to set up and solicit donations to help the needy families at Christmas. I mentioned before that our United Supreme Court is trying to move this country into a civil religion. A civil religion is a religion that excludes certain religious language. Sometimes significance of the sacredness of the Holy is too much for people to value in a noteworthy way.

The Star guided the wise men. These wise men were religious; they were pagan astrologers who studied the stars. These wise men were pagan seekers. They were not wise men; they were pagan astrologers whose divinatory skills were highly respected in the

Greco-Roman world. Their predictions had proven to be accurate. Many of the rulers feared the astrological signs. These wise men, as the Bible labels them, had been chosen by God to reveal the birth of the Savior to the world. He used these astrologers to teach us something about the Worship of the Savior. Astrology is the avenue God used to direct the wise men to the birthplace of Jesus. God has used pagan cities, customs and ideas and purified them to promote His purpose and cause of the Gospel. Worship is at the center of the Christian experience. It is a culmination of joy, adoration, pain, and sorrow. A.W. Tozer said, "God made us to be Worshipers." A.W. Tozer also said, "We are miserable without worship." In the book of Revelations we are told that we are created to worship Him. What can we learn from these pagan astrologers about worshiping God?

The **first lesson** we learn from these astrologers about worship is that there is a time to Worship God. When the time was right they journeyed from afar seeking to find the Christ Child with the purpose of Worshiping Him. When we come to church we should come with an attitude of worship. We should come with an aim to do nothing else but worship God. Worship time should be worship time not a time of gossip, not a time of joking, but worship. In worship we ascribe worth and value to God. Worship is a time when we give back to the giver. When we come to worship Him we come to worship Him, in spirit and in truth. Worship should not have to compete with entertainment. Entertainment is where we applaud one another, but worship is when we offer praise and thanksgiving to God not because of what He has done but because of whom He is.

The **second lesson** we learn from the astrologers about worship is that they came with a spirit of Humility. They fell down and worshiped Him. Their total being was involved in their worship. They realized that He was worthy to be worshiped and adored. Worship means ascribing worth and value to God. Worshiping God means more than just being present. We must avail ourselves to God by getting involved in worship. Worship is being intimate with God and showing God that we love Him. When we come to worship we must seek to sense His presence and have a sense of His holiness. When Isaiah went into the temple he sensed the holiness of God and cried out, "Holy, Holy, Holy, Lord God almighty heaven and earth are full of your glory." When we come before God as Isaiah did, we must have a sense of our unworthiness that we veil our faces, when we know that we are not what we ought to be. We must acknowledge His holiness by being reverent when we are in His presence in spite of our unworthiness. Worship enables us to experience the presence of God, but His power, His peace, and assurance that we are with Him and He is with us. Worship helps to keep us connected with God. Worship should draw us closer to God.

The **third and final lesson** we learn from these astrologers about worship is that they did not come to worship the Christ child with empty hands. Worship means not only that we receive but also that we give back to the giver. We give back to God when we worship Him. Many people want to take from God but they do not want to give back to God. They brought the Savior gifts. They presented Him with their treasures. They came and presented Him with Gold,

Frankincense and Myrrh. They did not come asking the Savior for anything, they came to bless Him. Bless the Lord O my soul and all that is within me bless His holy name. We give back to God in many ways. We should first give our lives back to Him and let Him be born anew in our lives. We should not only present Him with gifts, we should present ourselves before Him in an acceptable way. When we worship God through our giving we seek to give Him our best. When we worship God we give Him our full attention and we focus on Him. Worship should always be Christ centered and not self-centered. When one encounters God, as Isaiah did, he or she becomes quickened by the Spirit of God and has a readiness to serve God. He was ready to give of himself. We must take time, set aside time to worship God. He is worthy of our praise; worthy of our time; worthy of our tithe; worthy of our love, worthy of all honor and glory.

25

When Strongholds Turn Into A Stranglehold

(2Corthians 10:1-6)

Years ago the legendary Smokie Robinson wrote a song, "You Really Got a Hold on Me." In this song the lyrics stated that all he could do was think about the woman that really had a hold on him. The lyrics say, "I don't like you, but I love you seems I'm always, thinking of you, oh, oh, oh you treat me badly I love you madly you really got a hold on me, you really got a hold me, you really got a hold on me." This song describes how we find ourselves in situations that we know are not good for us, but they have such a hold on us we cannot break free. At some point in each of our lives we have allowed something or somebody to really get a hold on us and we cannot break free. Some of the holds that we have allowed have served to hinder us, hurt us or harm and keep us from being where God would have us to be. I am talking about the strongholds in our lives, and if they are not pulled down they can turn into strangleholds, which over a period time will destroy us if they are not dealt with and dismantled. There is much to be said about strongholds that turn into strangleholds if they are not broken. When we talk about strongholds we are talking about spiritual forces that are contrary to the will of God and the purposes of God. Certain bad experiences give birth to strongholds. Strongholds can be passed from one generation to another generation. Strongholds, if not dealt with and broken or destroyed, will turn into a stranglehold and when something has a stranglehold on you it will eventually destroy one both literally and figuratively. Many people have allowed strongholds in their lives to turn into strangleholds and it literally destroyed them. It is said that Howard Hughes, a millionaire, was of the opinion that everyone was out to steal his money. He became paranoid and would not eat and he depraved himself of food, thinking if he ate someone would poison him, therefore he died from starvation. The fear of someone wanting his money had a stronghold on him that turned into a stranglehold that led to his death.

The idea or opinion that someone was out to get him had such a stronghold on him that it turned into the stranglehold that drove him into insanity and he died. I remember counseling a family in which the wife had a stronghold of hostility toward her husband who had a child before they married. The wife acknowledged that her husband had informed her that there was a rumor that he had a child, but the woman had never informed him that it was true. The wife stated that he had been honest with her before they got married. The wife said that when they got married the woman sent papers from the court requiring her husband to have a blood test to verify that he was the father of the child. The wife went on to say she had allowed her hostility and anger over the years to ruin their marriage. The woman went on to confess that she had been advised by a friend that if she did not let her hostility and anger go it would destroy her marriage and it did. The hostility and anger that the wife held for years had a stronghold on her and it turned into a stranglehold, which over a period of time destroyed the marriage. Our text talks about the imaginations, meaning our thoughts. The mind is the first place the enemy will attack. There are some people who can get something in their mind and there is nothing you can do to change what they think. We can show them the facts and they still would not believe. That is why the scriptures say, "As a man thinks so is he."

What is a stronghold? A stronghold is a forceful, obstinate, stubborn argument, opinion, idea or a way of thinking that serves to resist the truth or the knowledge of God. A stronghold is a force that serves to hold something safely captive. A stronghold is like a castle or a fortress that's difficult to move. Strongholds are diametrically opposed to the knowledge of God. Listen to the text, "Casting down imaginations, and every high thing that exalts itself against the knowledge of God." This is how Satan deceived Eve, "And the Serpent said to the woman, ye shall not surely die: For God doth know that in the day ye eat thereof, then your eyes shall be opened, and ye shall be as gods, knowing good and evil" *(Genesis 3:4-5).* Satan sought to exalt himself against the knowledge of God. Anything that opposes Christ or the word of God is an enemy of the truth. Some people find protection and security in strongholds. Some people would rather stay the way they are instead of having the stronghold broken. They would rather say this is the way I am and I guess this is the way I will always be instead of making an effort to change. The sad part about a person having such a stronghold on them is that many say they are Christians. The way some people are, affects others, and if how I am or you are, is affecting others in a negative way, we need to make some changes. The Apostle Paul said, "If any man be in Christ he is a new creature, old things are passed way, behold all things become new" (*2 Corinthians 5:17*).

The **first thing** we need to understand about strongholds is that they will turn into strangleholds, if they are not dealt with or broken. We must understand that to deal with strongholds we must be prepared to wage war with them. Strongholds are ruled and governed by authoritative principalities. *(Ephesians 6: 12)* says, "For we wrestle not against flesh and blood, but against principalities, against powers, against rulers of darkness of this world, against spiritual wickedness in high places." The word "against" is used five times in this verse of scripture. One of the problems with Christians is their inability to identify the enemy. So often we fight against one another. The wife fights against the husband and the husband fights against the wife, and the children fight against the parents and the parents against the children, when the real enemy is not that person but the enemy that person is allowing to have power over them.

Our enemies are not natural, carnal or human, but spiritual. That's why the text says, "The weapons of our warfare are not carnal but mighty through God to the pulling down of strongholds." We cannot fight the enemy with carnal weapons such as knives and guns. Strongholds will turn into strangleholds if we do not know how to wage war against them. The difference between a stronghold and a stranglehold is the intensity of the grip. A stranglehold can destroy one quicker than a stronghold. A stronghold holds one captive as a prisoner but a stranglehold has intensity, which can instantaneously snuff one's life out in a few seconds. One can get strangled and choke to death if immediate action is not taken. A stronghold can slowly agitate one over a period of time. Then, all of a sudden it becomes a stranglehold and if not dealt with, it can cause one to lose their mind or self-control and they end up harming or hurting himself or herself, or another person.

The **second thing** we must understand about strongholds that can turn into strangleholds is that we need to know how to identify strongholds. We need to know how to identify strongholds like we need to know how to identify the enemy. One can know they are dealing with a stronghold when they see the same problem recurring in one's life that continues to keep that person down or causes that person to fail. When marital or family problems have not changed over a period of time, and have gotten worse, despite everything you have tried there is a stronghold of some nature that brings about constant failure. When a person has a propensity to keep making the same mistakes, there is a stronghold of some nature in their life. When something continues to happen in your life that is against the will and purpose of God, there is a stronghold that needs to be broken.

When a person is always in financial difficulty and they cannot seem to get any financial footing in their life and they always have to borrow, there is a stronghold at work in their life that affects their finances. Of course if we are robbing God and we say we are Christians something is wrong with our faith and commitment to God. The word says, "Will a man rob God, yet ye have robbed Me in tithes and offering. Ye are cursed with a cursed. But if ye bring your tithes to the storehouse that there may be meat in Mine house, and prove Me now here with, the Lord of hosts, and if I will open the windows of heaven and pour you out a blessing that ye shall not have room to receive, and I will rebuke the devourer for your sake and he shall not destroy the fruits of your ground; neither shall your vine cast her fruit before the time in the field, said the Lord of host" (Malachi 3:8-11). There are many forces in our lives that are against the will and purpose of God that are strongholds. Fear can be a stronghold, doubt can be a stronghold, rejection can be a stronghold, anger can be a stronghold, drugs can be a stronghold, sexual promiscuity can be a stronghold, lying can be a stronghold, jealousy and anything that is contrary to the will and purpose of God can be a stronghold.

The **third and final thing** we need to know about strongholds that can turn into strangleholds is that they cannot be broken with carnal weapons. Listen to the text; "The weapons of our warfare are not carnal, but mighty through God for the pulling down of strongholds." As Christians, we have spiritual weapons to wage spiritual warfare to pull down or break strongholds and prevent this from turning into strangleholds. Jesus himself showed us, when He was led by the spirit into the wilderness to pray and was tempted by Satan, how He had to use His spiritual weapons to defeat Satan. First, He who was the word knew how to use the Word of God to deal with the enemy. It is written He would quote to Satan. My brothers and sisters, if we are to pull down or break strongholds in our lives we must know the word of God and how to use the Word of God. When fear comes upon us, to defeat it, we must be able to say it is written, "God has not given us the spirit of fear but of power and a sound mind." We must know the word in order to speak the word where it says, "Fear not I am with thee, be not dismayed I am your God, I will strengthen thee, I will help thee, I will uphold thee with My righteous right hand" (Isaiah 43:10).

The Lord is my light and my salvation whom shall I fear, the Lord is the strength of my life, whom shall I be afraid" (Psalm 27:1). I remember early in my ministry I had a great fear of the dead. Whenever I would go to a funeral I would not be able to sleep for days. The fear of the dead was a stronghold on me. I talked with my father in the ministry regarding having this fear of the dead. He encouraged me to read (Psalm 119: 165) which says, "Great peace have they which love thy law and nothing shall cause them to stumble." Strongholds seek to hinder us from doing the work and will of God. When doubt comes, we must be able to speak to doubt and say, "I can do all things through Christ that strengthens me." When we feel rejected, we must speak to rejection and say, "For as many that have received Him to them He gave power to become the sons of God, even them that believe on His name." Pulling down strongholds that can turn into strangleholds means we need to get a foothold in the word of God and learn to speak the word persistently to the stronghold until it is broken and we are free. We must have faith in the word of God and believe that the word is powerful, that it breaks the power of the enemy and the power of canceled sin and sets the prisoner free. Strongholds are broken when we speak the word. Strongholds are pulled down when we speak the word. Strongholds are destroyed when we plead the blood. Jesus broke the stronghold of death when He died and rose again and said all power in heaven and earth is in My hands. I have the keys of both death and the grave.

26

The Three Principles of Faith

(Hebrews 11:1-10)

The bible would have us know that faith is essential and without faith it is impossible to please God. The scriptures tell us that the just shall live by his faith. This lets us know that faith is personal and subjective and objective. The "subjective" means the individual and the "objective" mean God. The scriptures tell us that we go from faith to faith, meaning faith is existential, and it is always in a state of becoming. Our faith is always in process. Our faith is always growing and being strengthen by the trials we face in life. The scriptures tell us that God has given to every man a measure of faith. We are to add to the measure of faith that God has given each of us. We live by faith, we walk by faith and we are saved by grace through faith. We have stated that there are five dimensions of faith. Faith is knowledge; faith comes by hearing, by hearing the word of God.

Faith is belief, if we can believe; all things are possible to them that believe. Faith is trust, trust in the lord with all thine heart and lean not unto thine own understanding. Faith is Obedience and hope; obedience brings the blessings of God and hope gives us substance to hope for the things we cannot see. Faith in God is the crown of life. Jesus spoke of the significance of faith in one way or another when He addressed healing and deliverance. He said to one man, "Be it done according to your faith." He said to the woman with the issue of blood that was healed when she touched the hem of His garment, "Woman thy faith has made thee whole."

He told his disciples on one occasion that they had little faith. Jesus said on another occasion, "That if one had the faith as a grain of mustard seed he could say to the mountain be thou removed and not doubt in his heart and it would be done." Then we see in our text, "These that all died in the faith, not having received the promises, but having seen them afar off and were persuaded of them, and embraced them and confessed that they were strangers and pilgrims on the earth." The scriptures teach us, "That faith without works is dead;" this tells us that there is a relationship between our faith and our works. Although we do not work for our salvation, we work by faith because of our salvation. The scriptures tell us that our faith should not be in the wisdom of men but the power of God. The scriptures tell us that our faith will be tested by trials. The scriptures tell us in (1Corinthians 12), that some people have been given the gift of miraculous faith. This kind of faith is what God has given to an individual who has the faith to believe that they can do great things for God. Jesus told His disciples that they would be able to do greater works than He would do. As we look at faith we see that faith in God enables the believer to live by his faith and to walk by his or her faith and to do God's work by faith. Let's notice a few men and woman of faith from the hallmark of faith in (Hebrews 11). "By faith, Sara received strength to conceive seed, and was delivered a child when she was of old age because God judged her to be faithful."

"By faith, Abraham, when he was tried, offered up Isaac: that he received the promise, offered up his only begotten son."

"By faith, Moses, when he was come to years, refused to be called the son of Pharaoh's daughter."

"By faith, when she had received the spies with peace, the harlot Rahab perished not with them that believed not."

Faith and faithfulness bring the blessings of God. One of the things we must understand about faith is that faith operates within certain principles. There are three principles we want to examine that govern one's faith.

The **first principle** that governs faith is the will of God. Jesus admonished His disciples that when they prayed to pray "thy will be done on earth as it is in heaven." God's will, will always overrule our will. In (Ephesians 1: 11), we read, "In whom also we have obtained an inheritance, being predestined according to the purpose of Him who worketh all things after the counsel of His will." The will of God involves God's purpose for us as well as what God wills for us, what God requests of us, and what God will provide for us. We need to understand that God's will and God's purpose work together for our good. God's purpose is what we have been created for that works within the will of God. Jesus Himself talked about doing the will of God. "Lo, I have come in the volume the book it is written of Me to do thy will O God." (Hebrews 10:7). When we ask God for something we must first seek His word to know if it is in His will. In First John it states, "And this is confidence that we have in Him, that, if we ask anything according to His will, He hears us: and if we know that he hears us, whatsoever we ask, we know that we have the petition that is desired of Him" (1 John 5:14-15). We have stated that when we are in the will of God we have His protection, His peace, His power, His presence, His provisions, and His promises. Being in the will of God affords us these benefits. Being in the will of God and doing the will of God brings the blessings of God and glory to Him. Faith works within the will of God for the believer. God's word is His will and His will is found in His word.

The **second principle** that governs faith is the grace of God. There is a relationship between faith and grace. By grace we have been saved through faith, which is the gift of God. Whatever we ask God for His answer is never without His grace. Grace is unmerited favor, meaning we are given what we do not deserve instead of what we deserve. We deserve judgment but God gives us mercy. We deserved hell but Jesus died that we might have life. We deserve death but God has given us life through Jesus Christ. We deserve to be abandoned but Jesus said, "I will never leave you, nor forsake, neither fail you." The Apostle Paul said, "I am what I am by the grace of God." Paul said to Timothy, "Be strong in the grace that is in Christ Jesus." "My grace is sufficient," said God to Paul, "For when I am weak, that's when I am strong, that the power of God may rest me." Our faith gives us access into the grace that God has provided us. (Ephesians 4:7) says, "But unto every one of us is given grace according to the measure of the gift of Christ." When the storms of life are raging and we feel that we are not going to make it, Christ Jesus our intercessor leans over to the Father and says Father give them a little more grace and still the storm for them. John Newton, a slave owner, talked about the grace of God one night when he was converted. He wrote that hymn, "Amazing Grace how sweet the sound that saved the wretched like me, I once was lost but now I'm found blind but now I see. Grace that taught my heart to fear, and grace my fears relieved, how precious did that grace appear the hour I first believed." Faith is the glove that receives the grace that God has given to each of us. There are seven truths about the grace of God. First, God's Grace comes through Jesus Christ. The law came by Moses, but Grace and truth came through Jesus Christ. Second, God's grace is sovereign; God gives His grace to whomever He pleases. Third, God's Grace is given to the humble. Fourth, God's grace is free, fifth, God's grace comes through faith, "By Grace we have been saved through faith." Sixth, God's grace is ministered by the Holy Spirit and seventh God's grace is sufficient. The grace of God takes us places that that our education will not. The grace of God opens doors for us that would be closed. The grace of God gives us friends who are in a position to bless us. The grace of God will make our enemies our footstool. The grace of God teaches us that if God is for us who can be against us. The grace of God reconciles us back to God through Jesus Christ. Grace restores, grace redeems, grace relieves our fears and grace leads us on.

The **third and final principle** that governs our faith is the timing of God. Everything that God has promised to do is for an appointed time. He told

Habakkuk that the vision was for an appointed time, though it tarry, wait for it, for it would surely come. God is not a man that He should lie or the son of man that He should repent. God's time schedule is not as our time schedule. He told Abraham and Sara that He would give them a child at an appointed time and it came to pass. Faith wins the victory at God's appointed time. Whatever we ask God for; if it's His will and He gives us the grace at the appointed time, it will come to pass. The will of God and the grace of God and the timing of God work together. There was a song we used to sing, "You can't hurry God you just have to wait, you have to trust Him and give Him time, no matter how long it takes. He's a God you cannot hurry." Job said, "In all my appointed times I am going to wait until my change comes." God's will and God's timing work together with the grace of God. Sometimes we think that something is God's will but it does not happen, and the reason it may not materialize at that time is because it may not be in God's timing. Sometimes it appears that the timing is right but if it is not God's will it still will not come to pass, but when God's will and God's timing and God's grace are working together, whatever we have been praying for, will come to pass. Whatever we have been waiting for will come to pass.

The story is told about a man and his son who needed firewood during the winter and they went outside and found a dead tree (they thought) and they sawed it down. In the spring, to their surprise, new shoots sprouted up around the trunk. The father said to the son, "I thought for sure it was dead because the leaves had all dropped in the wintertime." Everything around the tree was dead, so they thought.

The twigs snapped, but when they looked at the taproot there was still life. The father told his son that this was an important lesson for them: never cut a tree down in the wintertime or make any negative decision in the low times of life. He told him to learn to wait, be patient, the storm will pass, and spring will come. To everything there is a season and a time for every purpose under the sun. God has ordained all things in His own time. God knows what we need and when to give us what we need. We have to learn to hold out and hold on. He's an on time God. He may not come when you want Him but He will be there on time.

27

These Things

(Romans 8:28-39)

There are things that happen in life to us and around us that defies human reasoning. We are left with no understanding or explanation as to what has happened and the most we can say or the least we can say is that, "It's Just one of those things." I remember attending a funeral in Bessemer, Alabama where a young man I once pastored had drowned. While we were waiting in the pastor's study to go out and conduct the service, the question was asked, "What happened?" It was stated that the young man was a skillful swimmer and very athletic. They said they did not know if when he dived off the pier he hit his head and became unconscious or if he had gotten trapped beneath one of the piers and could not get out and he drowned. We pondered what could have happened; but no one knew the answer. One of the ministers said, "It's just one of those things." Here was a young man who was trying to live for God, who was an experienced swimmer, but mysteriously drowned. The church was on a picnic and this young man, who was a skillful swimmer, drowns, and all that could be said was, "It's just one of those things." We try to make sense out of the things that happen to us in relationship to God being in charge of everything, but in most cases all we can say when things happen to us is, "It's just one of those things." Sometimes we run the risk of thinking we are God or we can speak for God when mysterious things happen in our lives or the lives of others. There is the position, which says if God is all-powerful, all knowing and He loves us, why does evil exist? Why do bad things happen to good people? So at best, all we can say in reference to those things and some things that are inscrutable, things we cannot answer is, "It's just one of those things." Or if it's not one thing it's something else, or if it is not one thing it's two. Things will happen to us regardless of who we are. The Apostle Paul talks about these things: the things that confound us, the things that defy human reasoning, and the things that leave us searching for answers. He begins in verse twenty-eight of our text saying, "We know that all things work together for the good of them that love God and are called according to His purpose." We have to admit that some of the things that happen to us and around do not make sense according to human reasoning.

Throughout the bible we see mysterious things God allowed to happen to His people. God calls each of us for a purpose, and He has a purpose for each of us. God calls those that love Him and accept the call for a purpose. The call to Salvation and purpose is the call Paul is talking about. There is a relationship and a purpose behind the things that happen to us. The things that happen to us are not fortuitous. They do not happen by chance, or by accident. There are things that happen to us, such as the good and the bad, the bright the dark; the sweet and sour; the easy and the hard, the happy the sad; prosperity and poverty; health and sickness; calm and storm; comfort and suffering, life and death. These are some of the things that the child of God will have to experience and endure at some point in their lives. We remember the life of Joseph, a life that had been filled with vicissitudes and disappointments.

Then Paul in verse 31 says, "What shall we say to these things if God is for us, who can be against us?" When God is for us and He loves us, who will be able to stand against us? The things that come upon us, will they prevail against us if God is for us? They may try but they will not prevail because God is for us. They may cause some trouble but it will not triumph because God is for us. In verse 37 he says, "Nay in all these things we are more than conquerors through Him that loved us." Paul gives us a catalogue of the different things we face in life. What shall we say to these things? When you have tried and you failed and your best is not good enough. What shall we say to these things? Can we make sense out of these things? What can be said about these things?

In light or view of these things, the Apostle Paul mentions everything imaginable or possible as it relates to these things that attempt to separate us from the love of God. Paul says, "Who shall separate us from the love of God?" There are things the Apostle Paul talks about that confound us and defy human reasoning. When we examine the text, it appears that the answers to these things come before we discuss or identify these things. Paul talks about these things that confront us in light of Jesus Christ and His love for us. We see God's love demonstrated to us through Jesus Christ. "But God who spared not His own Son, but offered Him up, gave us His Son; will He not also freely give us all things?" Then Paul comes with three questions. Who will accuse God's chosen people? God declares us not guilty. Who will condemn them? Not Christ who died and was raised to life. Who will separate us from the Love of God? The Apostle Paul then asks, "What shall we say to these things?" Paul, in verse thirty-five, mentions a number of things in life that seek to separate us from God. Who or what shall separate us from the Love of God? God did not spare His Son of this world's troubles or trials. Shall tribulation? Shall trials, hardships, toil and other vicissitudes separate us from the love of God?

What shall we say to these things? It has been said that we live both under the shadow of God's judgment and under the light of His grace. But what shall we say to these things? Shall persecution separate us from the Love of God? When we have given our best and our best is not good enough. What shall we say to these things? When we have tried and failed. What shall we say to these things? When we look around and it looks like truth is on the scaffold and wrong is on the throne. What shall we say to theses things? When we look at how thousands of people were denied the right to vote or their vote did not count and the United State's Supreme Court overruled the recount in the Florida Supreme Court. The United State's Supreme Court decided who would be President. What shall we say to these things? Paul gives us a catalogue of the different things we face in life: tribulation, distress, persecution, famine, nakedness, peril, or sword. Can we make sense out of all these things? What can be said about these things? In light, or view, of these things, the apostle Paul mentions everything imaginable or possible as it relates to these things separating us from the love of God. What are we to learn from these things? What is God's purpose for allowing these things to happen to us? Why do bad things happen to good people?

The **first lesson we learn from the things that happen to us is,** "That all things work together for the good of them that Love God, and are called according to His Purpose." There is a redemptive side to the things that happen to us. God will use the things that happen to us to work things out according to the counsel and purpose of His will in our lives. The things that happen to us, God will use His wise counsel to only help us to help others. God knows the end from the beginning. Everything that has happened to us and will happen has a redemptive purpose. God will use the things that have happened to us, that are painful and disappointing, to work to our good, especially those that are called to fulfill His purpose. We, who are called to His purpose, have to be willing to open up our minds and see the redemptive side of the things that happen to us. The apostle Paul says in (Philippians 1:12), "But I would have you to understand, brethren, that the things which happened unto me have turned out rather unto the furtherance of the gospel." God works out everything according to His purpose. God's redemptive plan and his purpose work together for our good.

The **Second lesson** we learn is that there is a purpose behind the things that happen to us. Joseph could look back over his life, a life that was filled with persecution, disappointment and suffering, and could say to his brothers who were responsible for his misfortune, "What you meant for evil, God meant for Good." Joseph said to his brothers, "Now therefore be not grieved, nor angry with yourselves, that you sold me hither: for God did send me before you to preserve life, God sent me before you to preserve you a posterity in the earth, and to save your lives by a great deliverance" *(Genesis 45: 5&7)*. Joseph realized that God used him to fulfill a purpose. When we are called according to His purpose, He orders our steps.

What shall we say to these things? Job could say, "Though he slays me yet will I trust Him." We must know that God is going to make these things work together for our good. He is the one who allows certain things to touch us. He is the one who is ordering our steps. He is the one who says, "I know the plans I have for you, says the Lord, plans of peace, and not of evil, to prosper you and give you a future" *(Jeremiah 29:11)*. He is the one who is working behind the scene. He is the one who knows what it will take to make us into what He would have us to be. Job said, "He knows the way that I go and when He has tried me I shall come forth as pure gold."

The **third lesson** we learn from the things that happen to us is that God is perfecting us by the things that happen to us. Listen, "Nay in all these things we are more than Conquerors through Him that loved us." God makes us Victors and Heroes and not victims. We are conquering the enemy in the power of His might. The victory belongs to Christ, not us. The battle belongs to the Lord not us. God does not allow things to happen to us because He does not love us. God will use the things that He allows to happen to us as well as the things we play a role and part in to chasten us, because He loves love. "For whom the Lord loves He chastens, and scourged every son whom He receives" (Hebrews 12:6). God makes us, by the things He allows to prune and purge us; enabling us to become conquerors through Him that loves us. God has to sometimes break us in order to make us, and sometimes He has to empty us in order to fill us. God sometimes will reduce us or bring us to ground zero in order to rebuild us and to prepare us for greater works and greater challenges. There is an African Proverb that says, "Smooth seas do not make skillful sailors."

The **fourth and final lesson** we learn from the things that happen to us is that we have God's assurance. Paul said, "I am persuaded that neither death, nor life, nor angels, nor principalities, nor powers, nor things present, nor things to come, nor height, nor depth, nor other creature shall be able to separate us from the love of God, which is in Christ Jesus our Lord." The apostle Paul said, "For this cause I also suffer these things: nevertheless I am not ashamed: for I know whom I have believed, and am persuaded that He is able to keep that which I have committed unto Him against that day." Despite, and in light of, the things that happen to us we must have His assurance that if God be for us who can be against us. The Hebrew boys had this assurance and said, "If our God does not deliver us, it's not because our God is not able, for our God is able." Abraham had this assurance when he took Isaac up to Mount Moriah. When Isaac asked where the sacrifice was, Abraham replied, "The Lord will provide." God is able to do whatever we need Him to do to teach us, reach us, and meet us at our point of need. God has given us His assurance that He will always be with us. We must live with the blessed assurance that God is working out the things that we are experiencing. God is working out the things that confound us. God is working out the things that beset us. God is working out those things that overwhelm us. God is working out the mysteries in our lives and one day we will understand it better. We see through a glass dimly, but God sees and He is working it out for our good.

There are some things I may not know, there are some places I can't go, but I am sure of this one thing, that God is real for I can feel Him in my soul.

Yes God is real.

28

The Highest Level of Love

(Mark 12:28-34)

As Christians, we are admonished by Jesus to do many things that are difficult for some of us to do, and the one thing that is difficult for us to do is love others. As Christians, we are commanded to love one another as God has loved us. This can be difficult for some of us to do. To love, as Christians, is not a choice we have, it is a command. It seems impractical to love those who are our enemies, especially when our enemies have hurt us and have sought to despitefully use us. How can we love those who have openly and insidiously sought to harm us? The ethos and pathos, meaning the attitude and feelings of God, are found in His willingness to love us in spite of our sin. (Romans 5:8) tells us, "That God commended His love toward us in that while we were yet sinners, Christ died for us." Love is the essence of God; love makes God who He is and what He does. Some people do not know the power or the essence of God and His love. (Ephesians 3:17-18) tells us, "That Christ may dwell in your hearts by faith, being rooted and grounded in love, and able to understand what the breath, and length, and depth, and height and know the love of Christ." The one word that characterizes the height and the depth of the Christian life is "love". The word love is randomly used in the English language. It is a word we all use indiscriminately. Yet despite its random use, very few people know what the word really means when it is used. Often you hear a man or woman say, I love him or her, but I am not in love with them. Perhaps there is a difference between being in love and loving someone. Some people do not know what they are saying when they use the word love. Our text tells us that we are commanded to love God with all of our heart, mind, strength and soul, and thy neighbor as thyself, for there is no other commandment greater than this. When we hear and see people use the word "love" randomly and conditionally this tells us that there are different levels as well as types of love. One's expression of love says something about their ethos and pathos of love, meaning their attitude and feeling of love. How we use the word love reveals how we relate to one another.

The **first level** of love we want to examine is **Utilitarian** love. This love is conditional love. Someone loves you or you love someone because you can use him or her. This is the lowest type of love. Utilitarian love is selfish and seeks its own self-interest. The late Dr. Martin Luther King quoted the philosopher Immanuel Kant saying, "We must always treat a person as an end and not as a means." When you treat a person as a means, you depersonalize them. When we use people, they become things, not persons. Utilitarian love reduces people to things and depersonalizes them. This love not only reduces one but it also devalues one. Every person God has made has value and purpose. Our love for one another should not be based on our ability to use another person. This is not the highest level of love, but the lowest level of love.

The **second level** or type of love is **Eros love**. This is physical love between the two sexes. Sometimes Eros love is focused upon the good and the bad. It should be noted that Eros love is never used in the New Testament. It also deals with sexual passions between a man and a woman. This love is stimulated by the emotions and passions. This love is stimulated by how a person looks, moves, walks or talks. There is something about a person that excites one emotionally. However, this love is conditioned by what one can do for another person sexually, emotionally and physically. Shakespeare says, "Love is not love that alters when it alteration finds, or bends with the remover to remove. It is an ever fixed mark that looks on tempest and is never shaken. It's a star to every wondering bar." Eros love has an element of selfishness also. Eros love is motivated by one's emotions and passion that appeals to the physical. The meaning of love is not to be confused with some sentimental outpouring. Love is something much deeper than emotional bosh. Eros love has sentimental and affectionate value.

The **third level** or type of love is **Universal** love. This love is where we often hear people say I love everybody but they do not love anyone in particular. They never do anything to help anyone. They love in word, but not in deed. The bible teaches us to love, not only in word, but also in deed. Love is an action word. Love means to act, to do, and to respond to the needs of people. In (1 John 3:17-18) it says, "But whoso hath this world's good and seeth his brother have need, and shutteth up his bowels of compassion from him, how dwelleth the love of God in him. My little children let us not love in word, neither in tongue; but in deed and truth." This level or type of love is professed instead of put into practice.

The **fourth level** or type of love is **Philia.** This word comes from the word philanthropic. We also get the word Philadelphia. This love is a reciprocal and endearing love. This love cherishes. This is the love expressed between a husband and a wife for each other, of a brother for a brother, of a friend for the dearest of friends. It is the love that cherishes, that holds someone or something ever so dear to one's heart. We love those whom we like, and we love, because we are loved. We all need this kind of love and friendship from one another. We need friendships that we can value. We need friends that are trustworthy and reliable. Jesus told His disciples that they were no longer His servants, but His friends. He told them all the Father had revealed to Him. A true friend is someone you can confide in and they will not stand in judgment of you. This type of love is seen among fraternities and sororities. Men and women that belong to these types of groups or organizations engage in this type of love as brothers and sisters. This type or level of love is not the highest level of love because it is conditional and is restricted to a certain group or organization.

The **fifth level** of love is **Storge.** Storge is affectionate love. It is not mentioned or used in the New Testament. This kind of love exists between parent and child and between loyal citizens and a trustworthy ruler. This is also patriotic love for one's country. This love is not the highest level of love because it only exists between certain parties but does not transcend the parties.

The **sixth and final level** of love is the highest level of love. This love is **Agape love**. This love is the love God has demonstrated to us in Jesus Christ. This love is unconditional love. This love is redemptive love that's available to all mankind: an overflowing love, which seeks nothing in return. This love is the love of God operating in the human heart. At this level we love men, not because we like them, nor because their ways appeal to us, nor because they possess some type of divine spark. We love everyone because God loves the whole world. At this level, we love the person who does us an evil deed, although we hate the deed. This love is unconditional. This love is selfless and sacrificial love. The agape love is the love of the mind, of the reason, of the will. It is the love that goes so far, that it loves a person even if he or she does not deserve to be loved. It loves the person who is utterly unworthy of being loved. Selfless love is the love that God has demonstrated to each of us in Jesus Christ.

Moses told the children of Israel in (Deuteronomy 7:7-8), "The Lord did not set His love upon you, nor choose you, because you were more in number than any people: for you were the fewest of all the people. But because the Lord loves you; and because He would keep His oath which He swore unto your fathers." Christian love is not that you love for *your* sake, but we love others for *their* sake. We love because He first loved us. The Greeks and Aristotle sought the highest good and they found that the highest good was love. Love is the most powerful and durable force in the universe. God's love is unconditional and boundless. The late Luther Vandross said, "Any love." Tina Turner says, "What's love got to do with it?" The Fifth Dimension says, "Where is the love you said would be mine to the end of time?" The late Marvin Gaye said, "Your Love is all I need to get by." God's love, unlike all other types of love, is the highest level of love. God's love found a way to save man from his sins. Love was born in a lowly manger. Love will cover a multitude of sin. Love cast out fear. Love is patience, love is kind, love bears all things, believes all things. Love is not puffed up. Love hopeth all things, believes all things, endureth all things. Love never fails, but whether there be prophecies they shall fail. Whether there be tongues they shall cease, whether there be knowledge, it shall vanish away. And now abideth three, faith, hope, and love, but the greatest of these is love. Love called the prodigal son home. Love met the woman at the well. God's love has height, and width and depth and length. Love never fails.

29

A Faith Worth Defending

(Jude 1:15)

I want to use the words "defend" and "fight" interchangeably to make my point or to clarify my point. During the Sixties when the Civil Rights movement was going on Blacks fought non-violently for their civil rights. Through massive marches they were willing to contend for their right to vote. Through massive marches and rallies they marched non-violently defending their rights for equality and equal treatment. Many lost their lives as they marched for freedom and equality. Since that time things have changed dramatically. Many African Americans are not registered to vote and the many that are registered will not vote. Our value system has changed over the years. Our values are misplaced and the things we should value we devalue. Many people do not value the church, as did their fore-parents. Many people do not value their families enough to defend them. Fads and quick fix commodities have replaced our values. There ought to be something in every one's life that one values and is willing to fight to protect. It ought to be more than money. President George Bush has launched an attack on terrorism and said that we will defend and protect the freedom of the American people. The things we truly value in life are the things we will defend at all cost. But what about our faith, is it worth defending? In the sports arena, athletes will defend their titles. A boxer will train to defend his crown. Football or basketball or baseball teams will train to defend their titles, because being at the top means a great deal to athletes. It seems at times that everyone except Christians are willing to defend or protect what they believe. We come to our text where Jude is challenging the church to contend, defend the faith, which was once delivered unto the saints. Jude's initial plan was to write about one of the themes of salvation. But the Holy Spirit vetoed his initial theme and prompted him to address the theme of apostasy. There were many apostates who had crept into the church unnoticed. An apostate is one who has departed, or defected from the faith. An apostate was one who had heard and believed the doctrines delivered by the Apostles but had fallen away. The Apostles in the book of Acts laid the foundation for the early church and the scriptures tell us that the early church continued steadfastly in the Apostles doctrines and fellowship and the breaking of bread and continuing prayer.

The epistle of Jude sets out to tell the church why they should contend for the faith. The word "contend" means to defend, to defend the faith that was delivered. Jude told them to contend, defend the faith, because some, who were apostates, had crept into the church unnoticed. They had entered alongside someone else. They had slipped into the church from the side door. They had come in a side door. They had not come into the church when the invitation was extended for discipleship. They had not entered on their confession or profession of faith. Many men and women crept or slipped into the church because of who their mother or father was in the church. Perhaps a friend brought them into the church because they believed they would become a good member of the church. Just because a person is in the church does not mean that the church is in them. Just because a person works in the church does not mean that they are saved. We work because of our salvation not for our salvation. Our works do not save us, it's by Grace alone. "By grace are ye saved through faith, that not of yourselves, it is the gift of God: not of works lest any man should boast" (Ephesians 2:8-9). Many people have crept into the church and not acknowledged Jesus Christ as Lord and Savior. They came in the side door; they came in by professing one thing but believing something else. They did not come in the front door and declare their doctrinal position. This is the problem with many church people in the church. They will tell you that they believe in God but they cannot tell you what they believe. They will tell you that they believe Jesus died for their sins but they do not believe He is Lord over sin. They will tell you it's all right to sin; God will forgive you but they do not believe He can keep them from sin. He saves us from habits in our lives and will deliver us from sin if we ask Him.

Jude had to deal with the heresy of Docestism and Gnosticism. The Gnostics believed that the body was evil and the spirit was good. Therefore they believed that it did not matter what one did with the body. One was free to satisfy the lust of the body and practice blatant immorality publicly. Docetism was a doctrine whereby many denied that God was both God and man. They believed He was Divine but not human. Many had come into the church from the side door believing in Gnostism and Docetism. In (*John 10:1*) it says, "I say unto you, he that entereth not by the door into the sheepfold, but climbeth up some other way, the same is a thief and a robber." "I am the door," said Jesus. "By Me, if any man enter in, he shall be saved, and shall go in and out, and find pasture." We must believe that Jesus was God and Man. God the father, God the Son; Son of God and God the Son. Is your faith worth defending? What is it that makes one's faith worth defending?

The **first thing** that makes a faith worth defending is that it's a faith that has value. Living without faith in God is a defeated life. Charlie Rose asked the legendary preacher, Dr. Gardner Taylor, about his faith, and Dr. Taylor said that he did not see how anyone could make it without faith. In order for one to deal with life's trials and tragedies it is essential to have faith if one is to overcome. (Hebrews 11:6) says, "For without faith it is impossible to please Him: for he that comes to God must believe that He is, and that He is a rewarder to them that diligently seek Him." A faith that has value has to be pleasing to God. A faith that has value is authentic and not synthetic. An authentic faith has to be tested and tried by the vicissitudes of life. A faith that has value and is worth defending is resilient to life's trials and challenges. In the storms of life when all else fails our faith will sustain us if we value what we say we believe. A faith that has value is convicted by what it believes. In a faith that has value, value will not depreciate but will appreciate when it is tested and tested.

The **second thing** that makes a faith worth defending is that it's a faith that does not compromise when faced with persecution. An example of such a faith is that of Shadrach, Meshach, and Abednego when they were put in the fiery furnace; they demonstrated an uncompromising faith. They said to king Nebuchadnezzar, "Be it known to you O king that we will not serve thy Gods, nor worship the golden image which thou hast built. For if our God does not deliver us it is not because He is not able, for our God is able." A faith that will not compromise is unyielding. Faith, like love, endures, abounds, it increases in the face of persecution and will not relent. A faith worth defending will not compromise, will not bow, but will endure persecution.

The **third thing** that makes one's faith worth defending is a faith you are not ashamed to confess. In (Romans 1:16) Paul says, "I am not ashamed of the gospel: for it is the power of God unto Salvation to everyone that believes." Jesus said if you are ashamed to own Him before men, He will be ashamed to own you before the Father which is in heaven. The young high school student at Columbine in Colorado looked at her assailant who pointed a gun in her face and was not ashamed to confess that she was a Christian before she was killed. What a faith! The poet said, "O for a faith that will not shrink though press by every foe that will not bend or break against any earthly woe." One who says that he or she loves God cannot be ashamed to let their light shine before men. They cannot be ashamed to say Jesus is Lord, that He is King of Kings and the God of all Gods. A faith worth defending will not compromise when faced with moral decisions that will affect the lives of others. I once heard a former governor of Arkansas, when asked about his faith, if he was ashamed to let others know he was a Christian when he was at work. The governor replied that his faith was not something that he was ashamed of or something he wore and would take off when he went to work. A faith worth defending is a faith one is not ashamed to confess. Jesus said, "If I be lifted up from the earth I will draw all men unto Me" (John 12:32).

The **fourth thing** that makes a faith worth defending is a faith that yields results. Many people say that they have faith, but faith without works is dead. Many people say that they believe in God but they have no works to qualify their faith. Our faith is the root, but our works are the fruits. (James 2:21) says, "Was not Abraham justified by works, when he offered Isaac his son upon the altar." Abraham believed God and it was counted unto him for righteousness: and he was called a friend of God. To the Seven churches in Revelations the Angel said to all of them, I know thy works. If your faith is worth defending, it will yield results. It will yield fruits of repentance. A faith worth defending yields results. I remember when I was a prison chaplain and I ministered to many inmates who were from different faith traditions. I remember an inmate who was from a religion that branched off from Islam. I never tried to proselytize other inmates from other religions to become Christians. This particular inmate was later transferred to another institution after I left prison chaplaincy. One day I received a letter from him and when he closed his letter he said, "Yours in Christ." He would normally say El-Bey. He told me in the letter that one reason he went back to the Christian church was because I respected what he was practicing at that time and did not try to persuade him to change or attempt to condemn him or tell him he was wrong as other chaplains had done. The Apostle Paul stated,

"For though I am free from all men, I have made myself a servant to all, that I might win the more; I have become all things to all men" (1 Corinthians 9:19). If our faith is worth defending it should yield results.

The **fifth and final** thing that makes a faith worth defending is to know God is Faithful. Shadrach, Meshach and Abednego said, "Our God is able to deliver us." The Hebrew men knew that their God was faithful even when it appeared that they had no way out. They knew that God was faithful because He had been faithful in times past. (Romans 5:1) tells us that, "Therefore being justified by faith we have peace with God through our lord Jesus Christ." When we know God is faithful we have His peace and can be at peace in the midst of trials and tribulation "For tribulation works patience, patience experience, experience hope, for the love of God has been shed abroad in our hearts by the Holy Spirit. Our faith tells us God is faithful; He is the same today, yesterday and forever. God will not go back on His word. He is not a man that He should lie or the son of man that He should repent. God is faithful even when we are faithless. God will come through because faithful is our God. We are compassed about with so great a cloud of witnesses. Let lay aside, every weight and sin that does so easily beset us and run the race with patience, looking unto Jesus the author and finisher of our faith. God never fails, He abides with me, He gives me the victory because God never fails. Just keep the faith, never cease to pray, walk upright morning noon or night. He'll be there, there's no need to worry, because God never fails.

30

The Rock of Assurance

(Matthew 16:13-20)

The church has a guarantee on it that it will not fail. Its founder gives the guarantee; its author, its finisher and its perfecter have validated the warranty. We find these words in our text spoken by Jesus. He said upon the revelation of Simon Peter that He was the Christ, the son of the living God: that He would build His Church, and the gates of hell shall not prevail against it. The church has a guarantee that it will not fail, that it will succeed. He said that He would build His church. I recall hearing Dr. Gardner Taylor say we live in a day and age where people do not use the word Church anymore. They say worship centers, ministries. Jesus did not say that He would build centers or ministries. He said He would build His church. The church should have ministries that grow out of the church and provide services that meet the needs of people. He did not say that the church would not experience hardship or persecution. He said that the gates of hell would not prevail against it. We read in the book of the Acts of the Apostles where the church, at its inception, had to endure persecution, but, it did not fail. The hand of evil sought to terminate the church but it did not succeed. Evil served to advance the growth of the church and what was meant to hinder the church served to promote the growth of the church.

So the church has Gods' seal of success on it.

No one can say that it's his or her church. Jesus said, "He would build His church." No denomination can solely say that their church is the church Jesus was building. Jesus said in (St. John 10:16), "Other sheep I have that are not of this fold: them also I must bring." The church is a fellowship of believers; those that have been called out of darkness into God's marvelous light of grace and have entered into a Covenant relationship with God and the Church. The church has God's guarantee that it will survive, thrive and arrive. The church is in an existential state; it is always in a state of becoming. However, some of the elements are already in place. The foundation has already been laid. The Apostle Paul said, "Foundation can no man lay than that which is already laid, Jesus Christ." The Holy Spirit, which gave birth to the Church, came on the day of Pentecost. The church is built and sustained on two pillars: the death and the resurrection of Jesus Christ.

The church's assurance and guarantee is tied to Jesus Christ and not Simon Peter. Many people believe when Jesus said thou art Simon, son of Jonas that He was talking about Peter. They thought He was saying that the church would be built on Peter. Simon Peter gives no assurance or guarantee to the success of the church. Jesus said to Simon Peter that upon this rock He would build His church. Many people make the mistake thinking the church is built on people. The church belongs to God not to people. What rock was Jesus talking about? When we look in Malaysia we discover that in geology there are three different types of rocks.

The *igneous* rock is the **first rock.** Igneous rocks are crystallized from molten material called magma. This magma reaches the surface of the earth and flows over the igneous rock as lava. Because this rock can be overcome by the magma, it is not strong enough to stand against the gates of hell. Therefore Jesus was not talking about this rock. This rock could not withstand the gates of hell.

The **second rock** is called the *sedimentary* rock. The sedimentary rock is produced by the accumulation of material derived from the breakdown of preexisting rocks together with material of organic origin on the earth's surface. This rock cannot withstand the gates of hell because physical agents such as rivers, wind and rain can break it down through weathering, erosion and transportation of rocks. This rock is not strong enough to withstand the gates of hell.

The **third and final rock** is the *metamorphic* rock. Metamorphic rocks are formed by the alteration of igneous and sedimentary rocks. The metamorphic rock reaches a solid state when subjected to heat and pressure. This rock, under conditions of great pressure, will not only solidify but will also crumble under too much pressure. So this rock is not the rock Jesus was talking about. Well, some have said He was talking about Simon Peter. Jesus said to Simon Peter, "Thou Art Simon meaning pebble, stone meaning a little rock, Peter. You are a little pebble on the beach Simon Peter. I will build my church on the Petra, the bedrock." The church is not built on any personality other than Jesus Christ. Peter was only an Elder in the church. On one occasion Paul had to remind the church at Corinth that he, Apollos, and Cephas were just ministers. One-man plants, another waters, but God gives the increase. But Jesus said upon this rock I will build my church and the gates of hell shall not prevail against it. This rock is indestructible. Moses struck this rock in the wilderness. Daniel saw this rock coming out of Zion. Isaiah said Behold I lay in Zion a chief corner stone tried. This rock has been tried and proven to be stable. This rock is Jesus; He's the one. This rock is the Gospel the good news. The story is told about a storm that came to a city and knocked over trees and houses. In the aftermath of the storm there was a tree leaning to one side but it had not been uprooted as other trees had. When they were cleaning up the area and cutting up the trees that had been uprooted from their foundations they came to this tall oak tree and wondered why it was still standing. They begin to dig around the tree and as they dug they discovered that the roots of the tree were wrapped around a big rock. They determined that the rock had given the oak tree its stability when the storm came. Well, Christ is the rock that the church is built on and has sustained the church. David said when my heart is overwhelmed lead me to the rock that is higher than I.

On Christ the solid rock I stand all other ground is sinking sand. In every high and stormy gale my anchor holds within the veil.

31

What the Shepherd Does
for the Sheep

(Psalm 23/ St. John 10:11)

The Twenty-third Psalm is one of the most read psalms in the book of Psalms. This psalm is read frequently at funerals. It is very popular. There is a relationship between the Twenty-second Psalm, the Twenty-third Psalm and the Twenty-fourth Psalm. The three psalms are considered to be a trilogy. The Twenty-second Psalm speaks of the Good Shepherd. The Good Shepherd gives his life for the sheep. The Twenty-third Psalm speaks of the Great Shepherd. That great Shepherd of the Sheep, through the blood of the everlasting covenant, makes you complete in every good work to do his will. The Twenty-fourth Psalm speaks of the Chief Shepherd. When the chief Shepherd appears, you will receive the Crown of Glory that does not fade away. All three of these Psalms are considered the Shepherd's Psalms. In Psalm Twenty-two we see the Cross, in Psalm Twenty-three we see the Shepherd's Crux, and in Psalm Twenty-four we see the Crown, the King's Crown. In Psalm Twenty-two he is the Savior, in Psalm Twenty-three he is the satisfier and in Psalm Twenty-four he is the Sovereign: the all-powerful one. In Psalm Twenty-two he is the Foundation, in Psalm Twenty-three he is the Manifestation, and in Psalm Twenty-four he is the

Expectation. In Psalm Twenty-two he dies, in Psalm Twenty-three he is living, in Psalm Twenty four he is coming. Psalm Twenty-two speaks of the past, Psalm Twenty-three speaks of the present, and Psalm Twenty-four speaks of the future. In Psalm Twenty-two he gives his life for the sheep. In Psalm Twenty-three he gives his love to the sheep. In Psalm Twenty four he gives his light - when he shall appear. Psalm Twenty-three is more familiar than any passage of scripture in the Bible. All Christian groups and denominations are acquainted with Psalm Twenty-three. David wrote this psalm when he was an aged King. David the King never forgot David the Shepherd Boy. David wrote this psalm with a ripe experience. David reflected on his life as a Shepherd and wrote this psalm from experience. David was a man of war. He knew hardship, deprivation, and victory; he was tested and tried. The Twenty-third Psalm is known as the Great Shepherd Psalm. It speaks of the shepherd's love and providential care for the sheep. David compares his lord to that of a Shepherd who sets forth his love and care for his own sheep. David had been himself a keeper of sheep, and understood both the needs of the sheep and the many cares of a shepherd. It speaks of the shepherd's guidance and protection. What we see in this psalm is the relationship of the Shepherd and the sheep. It speaks of the ownership the sheep claim on the shepherd. David speaks with authority as he claims ownership. He speaks with authority; the Lord is My Shepherd. We must cultivate the spirit of assured dependence on our Heavenly Father. This is a declaration of faith, and a declaration of assurance. All believers should be under the pastoral care of the Great Shepherd. As we look at the condition of the world, what can this psalm tell us? As we face ominous signs of danger around us, what can this psalm tell us? There are always signs of war at home and abroad. Health-care for all working people is still being debated by congress and the president. The concern for social security is still a major concern. What can this psalm tell, that's so serene and peaceful, at such a time as this? This psalm speaks of calmness, peacefulness, green pastures and still waters. It speaks of God's providential care. This psalm tells us what the Shepherd does for the sheep.

The **first lesson we learn from** the shepherd is that the shepherd supplies the needs of the sheep. *I shall not want.* I may not possess all that I want; but I shall not lack for what I need: because the Lord is my Shepherd. Paul said, "My God shall supply all of your needs according to His great riches through Jesus Christ." *I shall not want* because the shepherd knows those things that we have need of before we even ask. The shepherd is able to supply whatever we need and He will meet us at our point of need. I shall not lack for temporal things because the Lord is my shepherd. I shall not want for spiritual things because His grace is sufficient. I shall not want because I have the skill or wit to win my bread, I shall not want because the Lord is my Shepherd.

The **second lesson we learn from** the shepherd and what he does for the sheep is; *He makes me to lie down in green pastures.* When I am exhausted he gives me rest in His word. His word is the green pastures; I am refreshed in His word. I find rest in His word. His Word allows me to lie down at night and rest peacefully. We find both rest and refreshment when we lie down in the green pastures of His word. When we are tired and weary He allows us to rest in the midst of the storms of life and keeps us until the storm passes over. And when the storm is raging, He speaks to the storms and says peace be still, and He tells us to be still and know that He is God. The word of God, which is green pastures, helps us to relax when we are troubled on every side. The green pastures give us His blessed assurance that all will be well.

The **third lesson we learn from the** Shepherd and what He does for the sheep is, *He leadeth me beside the still waters.* What are the still waters? His grace and blessed spirit attends us in various ways. His spirit renews us, cleanses us, and refreshes us. He leads us beside the still waters; we cannot go there by ourselves, we need His guidance. We cannot find the still waters; therefore, the shepherd has to lead us to the still waters. He leads us where there is peace and calm and serenity. The shepherd does not drive us; he leads us by His example. Savior like a shepherd lead us, much we need thy tender care. He leads us because we do not always know where to go. He leads us according to His word. He leads us by His spirit. He leads us not only through the valley but He leads us out of the valley.

The **fourth lesson we learn from** the Shepherd and what He does for the Sheep is, *He restores my Soul.* When the soul grows weary and sorrowful, He revives it; when it is sinful, He sanctifies it; when it is weak, He strengthens it. He restores my soul. When we would faint and grow weary; He gives power to the faint and to them that have no strength He increases their might. He restores my soul. When the soul's spirit feels disconnected with God: He restores the joy of my salvation, He restores my Soul. When I feel discouraged and feel my work is in vain; He restores my soul and says, "Let us not grow weary in well doing for in due season you will reap the harvest if we faint not." He restores my soul.

The **fifth lesson we learn from** the Shepherd, and what He does for the sheep is, *He leadeth me in the paths of righteousness for his namesake.* We are called upon in life to do the things, which will honor and please God. We are to honor our Great Shepherd by being a holy people, walking in the narrow way of righteousness. Our faith calls us to take both the high road and the low road sometimes. We are to do right by our families and neighbors. The paths of righteousness: we are to do right by the Church: the paths of righteousness. Whatever God may have us do, we must do it, led by his love: the paths of righteousness. When I was a boy, I won six banana splits. I thought I was supposed to eat all six banana splits. My mother would not allow me to have all six banana splits because I had six brothers and she made me share the other five with my brothers. My mother taught me what the paths of righteousness were all about. To do what is right is not always pleasant to do. We are to walk in the paths of righteousness and duty. We are to see that human rights are not violated in our communities, schools and country: the paths of righteousness. Not only in foreign countries, but right here in the United States: the paths of righteousness and the path of duty. *Yea, though I walk through the valley of the shadow of death.* This does not speak of death directly but of the shadow of death. We find ourselves walking through valleys that can lead to death. When our very being is tested we walk through the valley and the shadow of death. We not only walk in the valley, but through the valley. There are some people now who are walking through the valley of the shadow of death.

The **sixth lesson we learn from** the Shepherd and what He does for the sheep is; *thou preparest a table before me in the presence of my enemies.* If we were without enemies we might fear that we were not the friends of God. For the friendship of this world is enmity to God. In the presence of our enemies God feeds us, he protects us, and he sustains us. In the presence of our enemies we have the peace of God. The Lord prepared Joseph's table in the presence of his enemies. The Shepherd prepares our table in the presence of our enemies.

The **seventh and final lesson we learn from** the Shepherd and what He does for the sheep. Jesus said I am the Good Shepherd and the Good Shepherd lays down his life for the Sheep. The Good Shepherd was willing to become death eligible for you and for me. Greater love than no man has than this, that a man would lay down his life for his friends. The Good Shepherd gives His life for the sheep. The Lord is my Shepherd, I shall not want. He makes me to lie down in green pastures. He leadeth me: He restores my soul. Surely goodness and mercy shall follow me all the days of my life. And I shall dwell in the house of the Lord forever. The story is told about a young college student who was at church one Sunday morning and he asked the pastor if he could quote the Twenty-third Psalm. The pastor consented. The young man quoted the psalm very eloquently and never missed a verse. When the young college student finished quoting the psalm there was an elderly lady who got up and asked the pastor if she could quote the Twenty-third Psalm and the pastor consented. This elderly lady had broken language and stuttered as she quoted the psalm. When she finished quoting the psalm there was not a dry eye in the church. The question was asked what was different when the elderly lady quoted the psalm than when the young college student quoted the psalm. The difference, the pastor stated, was that the young college student knew the psalm but the elderly lady knew the Shepherd. He shall feed His flock like a good shepherd.

32

"God's Seven Spiritual Priorities"

Proverbs 3:1-6
Hebrews 2: 6-8

We live in a world where our priorities sometimes get misplaced. If we are not careful we can live our lives inverted, meaning we put last things first and first things last. As Christians, if our lives are not Christ-Centered, we will get our priorities misplaced. As Christians, God has given us an order for our lives and we are to subscribe to that order as well as come under that order, or else we bring chaos into our lives. God has given us spiritual order for our lives and this order comes under seven spiritual priorities I feel would bless and benefit our lives. There are seven spiritual principles written by Dr. John Cherry that help govern our lives. Some of these principles coincide with the seven spiritual priorities. The spiritual principle of organization is to simplify our lives. The spiritual principle of authority is to protect our lives. The spiritual principle of stewardship is to fulfill our lives. The spiritual principle of sowing and reaping is to provide for our lives. The spiritual principle of agreement is to crown our lives with peace. The spiritual principle of obedience is for God to bless our lives and the spiritual principle of unconditional love is to keep us from failing.

The **first spiritual priority** God would have us to fulfill is our relationship with Him. Attending church on a regular basis does not mean that one has a personal relationship with God. Worship is ascribing worth and value to God; we worship Him because of who He is not because of what He has done. A relationship with God involves intimacy with God, and intimacy with God involves spending time with God. We spend time with God when we study His word and spend time with God in prayer. We set aside time for prayer and study with God on a regular basis. One of the main ways we get to know God is through His word. The Christian's first priority is to put God first. (Matthew 6:33) says, "Seek ye first the kingdom of God and all His righteousness and all these things shall be added unto you." If we learn to seek God first then all the other things will fall in place. The Apostle Paul said, "That I may know Him and the power of His resurrection and the fellowship of His sufferings, being made conformable unto His death." One can never know Christ intimately without developing a personal relationship with Him.

The **second spiritual priority** that God has for our lives is for the family. Family in this sense means that the husband is to put his wife first. It is important that husbands and wives make each other a priority. The husband, mainly, should realize that according to the scripture he is to honor his wife as the weaker vessel. (1Peter 3:7). One thing that hinders or under minds the relationship between husbands and wives is being unequally yoked together. A believer should never marry an unbeliever. Light is not to have fellowship with darkness. It is important for the husband to be in right relationship with his spouse if they are to be in right relationship with God. There has to be spiritual agreement between husbands and wives. "Except two agree how can they walk together." Agreement for husbands and wives is built and based on the word of God. Agreement between husbands and wives brings peace to their relationship and the home. There are many husbands who are not under the authority of God and when one is not under the authority of God the relationship does not have the protection of God. The husband and the wife can only meet this spiritual priority when they make "God first" a priority and then one another.

The **third spiritual priority** for Christians to live by and make a priority is the children. (Psalm 127:3). One of the greatest crises in America is the abuse and neglect of children. There are many children in our country that are neglected and abused everyday. The best gift we can give our children is our time. The biggest mistake that many parents make is waiting too late to spend time with their children. Many parents are guilty of trying to satisfy their children by giving them things. I saw on the news some time ago where there were some parents who waited outside for twenty-four hours until a store opened to pay five hundred dollars for the new Play Station 3. Materialism and commercialism takes Christ out of the home. The story is told about the little boy who wanted his father to spend time with him, but his father made his career more of a priority than he did his family. The little boy's mother spoke to the father and told him that he needed to spend some time with his son, and stop promising him that he was going to buy him a baseball, bat and glove. The next time the father returned home from a business trip he honored his promise to his son. After buying him the baseball, the bat and the glove he told his son, "Now go play." The little boy went outside with his baseball, bat and glove and began to hit the ball against the wall outside of the house near his father's business room. The father began to become irritated with his son hitting the ball against the wall where he was working on business matters. Finally, the father got up and went outside and told his son, "I bought you a baseball, bat and glove; why can't you play and let me work." The little boy stated to his father that the baseball, bat and glove meant nothing to him if he didn't have anyone to play with. "Why can't you come out and play with me?" he asked.

T.V. Star Carroll O'Connell, whose son committed suicide, stated that he was too busy to spend time with his son when he was crying out for his attention. He stated that he had robbed and deprived his son of time with him, and now that he was gone he could not get those years back. Many parents have sacrificed time with their children for their careers. Our children should be a priority in our lives, especially during their developmental years.

The **fourth spiritual priority** God intends for all people and especially those who say that they are Christians is to be planted in a church. Anyone who says that he or she is a Christian and does not attend church is not fully connected with the body of Christ. (Hebrews 10:25) says, "Not forsaking the assembling of ourselves together as is the manner of some, but exhorting one another, and so much the more as you see the day approaching." Anyone who says that he or she is a Christian should be planted in a local church.

Every member has a place in the body of Christ. Every believer is to be connected with the body of Christ. The scripture says we are members of one another. When the body of Christ comes together there should be fellowship and the breaking of bread as we worship God. Every believer should be assembled with the body of Christ on the Lord's Day. The body of Christ represents Jesus Christ. The church is the family of God and we are His sons and daughters and brothers and sisters in Christ. For one to say that he or she is a Christian but never attends church is like a man saying that he is a fisherman but he never goes fishing. Being planted in a church says we are one with God and the body of Christ.

The **fifth spiritual priority** for our lives is living with a good work ethic. (2 Thessalonians 3:10) says, "If anyone does not work they should not eat." God ordained work when He made Adam. Adam had a job to do; he was to occupy the garden. When Jesus came, He said, "I must work the works of Him that has sent me for night comes when no man can work." God has given us all a job to do, at home and in the church. We are to abound in the work of the Lord as well as in our work to provide for our families. As Christians, our works are a reflection of our faith. "For faith without works is dead" (James 2:20). As fathers and men of God, we are to be industrious and innovative with the resources God has entrusted to each of us. We must work with our families, with one another and with God. We must work while it is day, for night comes when no man can work.

The **sixth spiritual priority** we are to live by is recreation. It is important that as Christians we learn to take care of our bodies. We should not just work and eat all the time and never relax. Many Christians fail to take care of themselves physically or emotionally. (1Timothy 4:8) says, "For bodily exercise profits little; but Godliness is profitable unto all things." Bodily exercise does benefit us if we take time to exercise properly. As Christians, we are to keep our bodies as fit temples for God to dwell in. God is growing us into His likeness; unto the full stature of the man Christ Jesus, into a perfect man. It is sad that so many Christians are over weight. We must preserve the body, the temple of God. We must become better stewards of our health. God is a healer, but the sole responsibility does not rest upon God when it comes to our health. The late Dr. Martin Luther King said, "The belief that God will do everything for man is as untenable as the belief that man can do everything for himself. It too, is based on a lack of faith. We must learn that to expect God to do everything while we do nothing is not faith, but superstition." The scriptures state that God desires, above all, that we prosper and be in good health even as our souls prosper.

The **seventh and final** spiritual priority we must incorporate in our lives is rest. There comes a time when we need to rest from our labors during the week. In the book of Genesis we read that after God had created the heavens and the earth and ordered each day and stated that his works were good, He rested on the seventh day. We need rest - emotionally, mentally, physically and spiritually. In the arena of life we become drained, and unless we rest, we cannot become rejuvenated and renewed to face life's ongoing challenges. Over the years I have learned to rest and relax and know that God is in control. The scriptures say, "Rest in the Lord and wait patiently for Him"

(Psalm 37: 7).   We need to rest in the word of God when we feel overwhelmed. We must rest in His promises when we feel that we cannot last another day. We must rest our minds and know that He has promised to keep us in perfect peace if we keep our minds stayed on Him. When we are down, Jesus said, "Come unto Me all ye that labor and are heavy laden and I will give you rest, take My yoke upon you and learn of Me, and you shall find rest."

33

God's Hidden Treasure

Genesis 1: 26
2 Corinthians 4: 1-16

All too often we are guilty of discounting ourselves as well as others. I am guilty of discounting myself when others pay me a complement. Often I say in response to a complement, there isn't much to me. Sometimes we say that others are nobodies. We often devalue ourselves as well as others. The bible says, as a man thinks so is he. If we would not devalue ourselves others would not devalue us. The truth for some of us is that we do not count for very much. We are not dependable or reliable. We are subject to change our loyalties. Sometimes, when we say there isn't much to people, we can make a pretty good case for our argument. Some people, when things do not go their way, become angry and hostile. We have all been gullible, foolish and guilty of doing stupid, shameful things. However, there is more to us than we often give ourselves credit. We have this treasure in earthen vessels. There is more than what is low and sleazy and cheap in us. We have this treasure in earthen vessels. There is something august and splendid and like God in each of us. In the beginning we are told that we are made in the image and likeness of God. "Our faith tells us that that we are the children of God and it does not yet appear what we shall be.

But when He appears we shall be like Him." We are not yet completely made, but we are being made in the image of God. God is growing us into the full stature of the man Christ Jesus, into a perfect man. We are not there yet, but we are in an existential state, a state of becoming. We never cease to become, while we are in these vessels. It has been said that in the worse of us there is some good, and in the best of us there is some bad. We are not all bad and neither are we all good, but there is a treasure in the worse of us. I have often heard someone say there is a treasure in everybody. There is some good in everybody and a great deal of honesty and friendliness and decency in people around us. But whatever good is in us, it is not in and of ourselves, it's the God in us. There is some of God in each of us, because we are made in the image and likeliness of God. Langston Hughes has written a novel entitled "*Tambourines to Glory.*" Much of it is a caricature of what is cheapest and ugliest in the ghetto. The main theme of the novel is the description of how people are victimized by racketeers in religion with their prayerful pay principles, and too much of it is true, though revolting. There is, however, a high peak in the book; a partner in a new cult in Harlem, touched with the awe and holy aspect of religion, says religion has got no business being made into a gyp game. Whatever part of God is in someone is not to be played with; everybody has a part of God in them. The bible says we are made in the image and likeness of God. It says that we humans are not just entities that happened, strange characters not in the script of creation's purpose, which just happened to wander on stage. The Apostle Paul would have us to know that we have a treasure in our earthen vessels. God chooses to use earthen vessels to do His work. It does not matter who we are, we are God's earthen vessels. The power is not of us, it is of God. This is the paradox of the gospel treasure. God chooses to involve man in His divine plan and purpose. God allows His light and His love to shine through earthen vessels. We are God's earthen vessels. A vessel is a container or instrument that God uses to fulfill His purpose. As vessels, we allow ourselves to be marred by sin. Sin has a way of destroying the vessel if we are not careful. Drugs and alcohol and other immoral propensities will destroy this earthen vessel. However, when we become children of God by accepting Jesus Christ as Lord and Savior, He recreates us, and we are His workmanship created for good works. The word "workmanship" means we are His masterpiece. God, who came to us in Jesus Christ, has redeemed us from the curse of the law and has placed His treasure in each of us. As vessels we are instruments in the hands of God.

The **first thing** we must understand about being an earthen vessel is that the vessel is only an instrument that God uses. The Greek word for "earthen" is ostrakinos, meaning clay vessel. We are weak clay vessels, pottery that can be broken. A vessel has no power; it is only an instrument or vessel that God uses. "But we have this treasure in earthen vessels." The Apostle Paul says, "That the excellency of the power is not of us but of God." As vessels we have a tendency to feel that we have all the power. Some people feel or think what they say goes. This is not always true when it comes to God's work. This was the awful mistake King Saul made. He forgot that he was an instrument in the hands of God. He forgot that God made him a king; he did not make himself a king. God has never a made a human vessel that is indispensable. Moses was a vessel God used but he was not indispensable. God used Joshua to lead the children of Israel into the promise land. David was a vessel that God used but he was not indispensable. God used his son Solomon to build a house for the Ark of the Covenant.

It is told that a bishop in the A.M.E. Zion church, at a general conference or board of bishops meeting, fought a resolution. It is said that he made the comment that the only way the resolution would pass would be over his dead body. He left the meeting angry and dropped dead. The word of God says it's not by power or by might but by my spirit says the Lord. The Apostle Paul stated, "That the power may be of God and not of us" (II Corinthians 4:7). As vessels and instruments of God we must remember that God has the final say so in all matters. God can veto any decision or vote if He wants to. We are His workmanship created in Christ Jesus for good works. We are the works of His hands not the works of our hands. One of the great temptations and failures of man is to think that he or she is more important than what God has called us to do.

The **second thing** we must understand about a vessel is that it must first be broken before it can be used by God. The story is told about a young opera singer who sang so melodiously, but a professional opera singer noticed that her voice was not quite refined. The older singer told the young singer that when her heart was broken she would sing with a different note. As earthen vessels we have to be broken before God can use us. We want to mold ourselves instead of allowing God to mold us. He some times has to break us in order to mold and make us. The idea of the vessel being broken comes from (Judges) the seventh chapter. Each man had a trumpet and a torch and a pitcher or an earthen vessel. They carried their torches in the earthen vessels so that the light could not be seen from a distance. When they got among the Midianites they broke the earthen vessels. It was not until the earthen vessel was broken that the light could shine out. The problem with many people in the church is they haven't been broken. Some people need to be broken of pride, jealously, envy, disobedience and self-righteousness. It is when we are broken that the light of God's love shines through us, not before. Some people can pretend to be Christians, but Jesus said, "By your love men will know that you are My disciples indeed." When we are broken, the light of God's peace, joy and strength shines through us. We have this treasure in earthen vessels.

The **third thing** we must understand is that it is the treasure that gives value to the vessel. It is the God in us that gives our vessel value. He gives us value and worth in spite of our feelings of worthlessness and helplessness. He sets His affection upon us. His power finds its full scope in human brokenness and weakness. It is His breath and air that made us a living soul. We are because God is; we are because He is in us. It is Christ in us, the hope of glory. We are not made, we are being made, and sometimes it takes some heartaches, and heartbreaks, and disappointments, and struggles before God can get any glory out of our lives. God has to put us on the anvil and sharpen us with iron. Iron sharpens iron. God has to sometimes show us tough love, as a parent has to show a child.

The **fourth and final thing** about the treasure is

that it is priceless and does not cost us anything. You cannot buy this treasure; it's not for sale. You have to believe and accept Jesus as your personal Savior. You have to accept that He has accepted you. You have to accept your acceptance. Paul had this treasure, Peter had this treasure, John had this treasure, Silas had this treasure, Timothy had this treasure, his grandmother had this treasure, and his mother had this treasure. The story is told of a legend in the biography of Michael Angelo, the great sculptor who painted the sixteenth chapel on the Vatican ceiling. While walking along the street, Michael saw a rude, ugly stone, misshapen and dull. He picked it up and carried it in his bosom to his studio. A friend asked him as he worked on the stone, "What it is that you see in this ugly mudded stone?" Michael replied, "I see an angel in the stone." Michael began beating the stone with his chisel and his mallet and lumps of the stone fell off. Particles began to separate from the stone. He was loosing the angel in the stone. When he was finished, what had been disfigured and ugly became perfect in symmetry, flawless in its features. A magnificent sculpture, an angel had come out of the stone. Well, there is not much in you and me, but we have this treasure in this flesh that we dwell in. God preserves us because of the treasure within us.

The treasure within us enables us to endure trials and tribulations. We have a transforming power within us that keeps us from falling. When we fall, He that is in us, picks us up, tells us that He still loves us, offers us His forgiveness and gives us a second chance. We have this treasure and one day we will stand in the beauty of His holiness and the holiness of His beauty. Thanks be to God we have this treasure.

We have this hope, we this peace, we have this joy, we have this strength, we have this power, we have this light for darkness, and this assurance that though the outward man perish, the inner man is renewed.

Jesus paid it all, all to Him I owe, sin has left a crimson stain He washed it white as snow.

About the Author

☐

Pastor Wayne B. Murdock attended three Institutions of higher learning to attain his ministerial credentials. The first was Clark Atlanta University in Georgia, where he attained his Bachelor of Arts Degree in Religion and Philosophy in 1985. He graduated Magna Cum Laude. The second was Emory University in Atlanta, Georgia, where he attained his Clinical Pastoral Education (CPE) training in 1998. There he completed a Basic Unit of CPE and one advanced year of residence training at the Athens Regional Medical Center through Emory affiliated hospitals, totaling five units. The third Institution was Erskine Theological Seminary in Due West, South Carolina, where he received his Masters of Divinity Degree. At the church he founded, he pioneered a "Boyz to Men Mentoring Program," for young males at risk. He also implemented other ministries that will empower the lives of others in the community. Pastor Murdock is an achiever and has several accolades within his repertoire. In 1987 he was the recipient of the *"Outstanding Young Men in America Award."* In 1994 he received the *"Spark Award"* from the Prison Fellowship Ministry for leading a Community Project in Cabarrus County. Also in 1994 he was the recipient of the *"Frederick Douglass Memorial Award"* for Community Outreach. The late Bishop Ruben L. Speaks bestowed this award on behalf of the West Central North Carolina Conference of the African Methodist Episcopal Zion Church while serving there as a pastor. In 1997, as president of the Cabarrus County local chapter of NAACP in Concord, North Carolina he was awarded the *"Drum Major for*

Justice Award" for his vision and leadership. He served on the Board of Directors of Hospice in Cabarrus County, Concord, NC. He has worked as an Intensive In-home Coordinator/ Counselor/ Therapist / Clinician and now works as a Clinical Coordinator and a certified trainer for Therapeutic foster for therapeutic foster care for Community Specialized Services, Inc., Concord, NC. He works as a Residential Counselor/Intervention Specialist for the Nazareth Children's Home in Rockwell NC. He humbly serves his community as chaplain and board member of the Guildford County Interfaith Hospitality Network and is a member of the High Point Minister's Conference in High Point, NC. Pastor Murdock will have conferred upon him the Honorary Doctorate of Divinity degree from Erskine College and Theological Seminary located in Due West, South Carolina. May 16th 2009 for his distinguished career in ministry and human services.

Sources and references

Bible, King James Version

Strong's Exhaustive Concordance
James Strong, LL.D, S.T.D.

Commentaries by
Dr. J. Vernon McGee

The Interpreters Bible

Quotes by Dr. Martin L. King

Dictionary of Theology,
Karl Rahner/Herbert Vorgrimler

Dictionary Concordance
Holman Christian Standard Bible

The Names of God
Lester Sumrall

BLACK INK PUBLISHING

Attention Writers

Black Ink Books is currently seeking new authors of urban fiction including poetry, testimonies and autobiographies.

All manuscripts should be addressed to:
Dynasty Publishing
Black Ink Books
Attn: Submissions
5585 Central Ave
Charlotte, NC 28212

Let us help you put your story into print!